Country Stenciling

Easy, Beautiful Designs for Your Home

Contributing Designers

Barbara Robins & Cynthia Willoughby, L.A. Stencilworks

Nancy Tribolet, Stencils by Nancy

Leanne Watson, Primitive Designs

Publications International, Ltd.

Contributing Designers & Writers

**Barbara Robins & Cynthia Willoughby,
L.A. Stencilworks**
Barbara Robins and Cynthia Willoughby have owned
and operated L.A. Stencilworks since 1998. Barbara
Robins began her career as a decorative artist in the
early 1980s. In 1987, she was awarded a Certified
Decorative Artist Certificate from the National
Society of Decorative Painters. Ms. Robins designs all
of the stencils for the company. Cynthia Willoughby
started her decorative painting business in Southern
California in the late 1980s. Ms. Willoughby teaches
stenciling throughout Southern California and
stencils all of L.A. Stencilworks' designs and murals
for the company's catalog and Web site.

Nancy Tribolet, Stencils by Nancy
Nancy Tribolet has been a professional decorative
painter for over 20 years. She has written numerous
magazine articles and instructional books. She designs
stencils for her custom stencil business, Stencils by
Nancy, which she has owned and operated since
1990. She is a member of the Stencil Artisans League,
the National Society of Decorative Painters, and the
Society of Craft Designers. In 1988, she was awarded
a Certified Decorative Artist Certificate from the
National Society of Decorative Painters.

Leanne Watson, Primitive Designs
Leanne Watson owns and operates Primitive
Designs, a company she started in 1999. She designs
all of her stencils, which capture a primitive, country
feel. Both stencils and finished crafts can be purchased
through the Primitive Designs catalog and Web site.

Contributing Writer

Susan Villas Lewis is owner of The Fab Faux, a
residential and commercial decorative painting
business in Carrollton, Texas. She holds both a
Bachelor and a Masters of Arts degree in journalism
and is a member of the Stencil Artisans League.

Photography

Photography: Silver Lining Digital, Inc.
Photo Shoot Consultant: Merilee Sawusch
Photo Shoot Stylist: Charlotte Lyons
Hand Model: Monica Kowallik/Royal Model
Management

Louis Weber, CEO
Publications International, Ltd.
7373 North Cicero Avenue
Lincolnwood, Illinois 60712

Permission is never granted for commercial purposes.

Manufactured in China.

8 7 6 5 4 3 2 1

ISBN: 0-7853-6282-7

Library of Congress Control Number: 2002102207

Table of  Contents

Welcome to the World of Stenciling

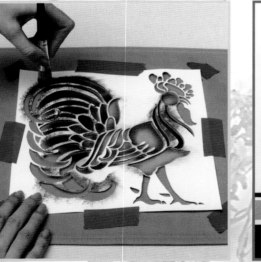

What is stenciling? Stenciling is an age-old technique in which paint is applied to a surface through a cut-out template. Designs can be repeated or used alone to achieve a consistent pattern with a handmade feel. Modern twists to the traditional craft have opened the door to even greater personal style and artistry. With simple step-by-step techniques that are easy to learn and master, walls and accessories can be transformed to suit your taste and to create harmony in your rooms. Another bonus of stenciling is that you're able to create one-of-a-kind looks without spending a lot of money. There's no limit to what you can do with stencils!

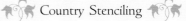

Stenciling Tools

Single-overlay stencil

Multiple-overlay stencil

When marking registration points, make a mark through each hole on the first overlay; match up the marks on subsequent overlays.

Most stenciling supplies can be found at local craft and hobby stores, though you might need to check a hardware or home improvement store for tools such as a level or tape measure if these items aren't already stocked in your toolbox. A wide variety of detailed stencils, high-quality brushes, and other accessories can be found in stencil catalogs as well as online.

Stencils

Stencils are typically made from a stiff plastic called Mylar (a material that's sturdy enough for repeated use and that cleans up easily), though brass, coated paper, and acetate can also be used. They come in two basic types: **single overlay** and **multiple overlay.** This simply refers to the number of stencils required to get a complete image.

A single-overlay stencil is made up of one layer. These designs are usually simple and have obvious spaces, called bridges, between each part of the image. The bridges create distinct shapes that make up the design; without them, you would see just one big shape and no details! Although pictures that are created with a single-overlay stencil will never be completely realistic, these are good stencils for the beginner. They are easy to apply, allowing you to develop a working technique. As your skills advance, you can make even single-overlay stencils look more complicated by blending colors, freehanding details, and masking off areas to separate colors for a more realistic effect.

Multiple-overlay stencils allow for more realism because painted areas butt right up against each other rather than being separated by bridges. One single design is cut on multiple stencil sheets, as the name implies, with different areas on each overlay. Color is added one layer at a time until the image is complete. The size and detail of the image determine how many layers there are to the stencil. The overlays are matched up with registration marks.

Registration marks are usually little holes in the corners of the stencil; make a pen or pencil mark through each hole on the first layer, then line the holes up with the marks on subsequent layers.

Brushes and applicators

Stencil brushes, the most common applicators, have short, stiff bristles of uniform length and come in a variety of sizes. Handles range from straight wood to plastic bulbs; find what's comfortable for you. You will need several brushes, ideally one for each color used. This keeps colors from becoming muddy and also speeds things up because you won't have to clean your brush between colors.

Match the size of the brush to the size of the area to be painted: Ideally, the brush should be about half the size of the area to be painted. This helps contain the paint in the correct areas without having to mask the rest of the stencil. If the whole stencil will be one color, use a bigger brush, which allows you to work more quickly. But if you need to apply a specific color to one tiny area, use a smaller brush to keep the paint where you want it. Also use

An array of brushes and applicators

smaller brushes for adding shadows and highlights.

To obtain different looks, experiment with other applicators. Sponges, which give a less filled-in look, may be cut down to a workable size. Rollers can speed up the project greatly but don't allow for subtle shading or detail. Cotton swabs, cotton balls, cheesecloth, sponge brushes, and spray paint provide unique looks as well.

Paint

There are two basic kinds of paint used in stenciling: acrylic and oil. **Acrylic paint** cleans up with soap and water and comes in a wide variety of colors that can be easily mixed to make others. Acrylics dry quickly, so paint doesn't smudge easily. Shading is created by adding other colors on top of the base-coat rather than blending the colors.

However, because acrylic paint is very liquid, it is easy to get too much paint on the brush, causing seepage under the stencil.

Trick of the Trade: To keep brushes workable while stenciling with acrylic paints, load them with gel blending medium and work them on paper towels to clean and soften.

Oil paint comes as crèmes and crayons. These take longer to dry, making them ideal for blending and creating smudgy shadows. They're less likely to run under the stencil because of their solid state, but they come in a smaller number of colors and cleanup is more difficult, requiring mineral spirits or brush cleaner. You need to stencil with oil-based paints on an object that has an oil-paint basecoat.

Trick of the Trade: Be careful when stenciling, but if you do notice any smudges, you can do touch-up work on oil paints with a white art gum eraser.

Adhesive

Adhesive spray or tape holds the stencil in place. Most of the time, tape is the easiest way to adhere a stencil. It's also useful for masking off areas of the stencil you don't want to paint yet. Low-adhesive tape works best, because it adheres well yet won't mar the surface or pull off the paint when it's removed. Keep plenty of low-adhesive tape on hand for every stenciling project.

Trick of the Trade: Make standard masking or painter's tape a little less sticky by sticking it to your shirt before putting it on the stencil.

Although spray-on, repositionable adhesives are a little more expensive, messier, and smellier than tape, certain situations call for their use. On a smooth, slick surface, for instance, spray adhesive can be helpful in keeping paint from seeping under the edges of the stencil. Spray adhesive is also ideal for stenciling on tricky or hard-to-reach areas such as ceilings or curved surfaces.

Trick of the Trade: Before using a spray adhesive, make sure your work area is well ventilated.

Palette

When stenciling with oil-based paints, you'll work out of the crème pots they come in. But when working with acrylics, you'll need to place the colors on a palette. Palette paper is sold in craft and art stores for this purpose, but paper or foam plates work just as well. You can also try a piece of matboard or cardboard or even an ice cube tray! Just make sure that whatever you use is big enough to keep the colors separated.

Other tools

Depending on the project, there are a few other items that prove indispensable when stenciling. It would be wise to keep all of them on hand.

Art gum eraser. This tool is useful when working with stencil paint crèmes. Because these paints dry slowly, minor smudges and mistakes are easily wiped away with a white art gum eraser.

Artist's brushes. Use these small, thin brushes to add details like shadows or leaf veins.

Index cards. These make handy masking tools for small spaces.

Level. This common tool helps keep a border straight.

Paper towels. Use them to wipe excess paint off brushes, to protect surfaces, and for general cleanup. Keep a roll nearby while you're working.

Pencil. Use a pencil for marking level lines and registration marks.

Tape measure. Keep one on hand, or a ruler if you prefer, to determine the amount of space available for the stencil when planning projects.

A variety of paints

Paint colors should not touch on the palette; use a paper towel to offload excess paint.

Surface Issues

With proper preparation and the correct type of paint, almost any surface can be painted. Paint manufacturers are coming out with new formulas all the time, making it easier to carry a decor theme through on almost any item you wish. Here are a few of the different surfaces (other than walls!) you might paint on.

Glass and ceramics. Use paint meant for glass and tile. It comes in transparent colors for a stained-glass look as well as opaque shades. When stenciling glass dishware, paint the bottom of the plate or the outside of glasses rather than the surfaces food will come in contact with. Follow manufacturers' directions for setting the paint.

Fabric. Paints designed especially for fabric will stay soft and wear better than regular paints. The softness of the paint is less important on items that won't be worn, such as curtains. To stencil on fabric, use spray adhesive and tape the fabric down well. Put a piece of cardboard or waxed paper under the fabric to prevent the paint from soaking through. Build up color slowly, as the paint can wick under the stencil if you use too much. Follow manufacturers' directions for heat-setting the paint and washing the fabric.

Trick of the Trade: If you can't find the color you want in a fabric paint line, add a textile medium to regular acrylic paint.

Paper. Consider using inks or pigment dyes instead of paint to apply a stencil on paper. These are drier and won't soak into the paper as much. If you must use paint, try painting a basecoat first to stabilize the surface. Then stencil as usual.

Metal. There is a line of paint designed for use on metal without priming, but if you need a color not available in this metal paint, remember to prime the surface first. Otherwise, the paint won't stick.

Wax. To stencil on candles or soap, start with a special conditioner, then use paint developed specifically for this surface and follow manufacturers' directions.

Choosing a Design

Stencils come in a wide variety of sizes, shapes, and styles. The stencils in this book are just a starting point as far as design goes. Commercially available stencils mimic all kinds of animals, plants, flowers, architectural details, and more. Start by deciding what type of image you're interested in, then look at the style and scale of your options.

Size. The stencil needs to be the right size for the application. A 2-inch-wide stencil wouldn't carry enough weight for a border at the top of a 12-foot wall, but it might be just right to trim a tablecloth. A 20-inch spot motif wouldn't be appropriate for use on a wastebasket, but it can top off a window quite well.

Shape. Long, narrow stencils are usually meant as borders rather than center medallions. Many stencils are fluid in their shape: You can rearrange the elements to create a new shape, and thus a new use for the stencil.

Style. The style of the stencil is another checkpoint in choosing a design. This book covers country stenciling, encompassing a wide range of styles from primitive to French to farmhouse. Before you begin, make sure the design you choose works with the style of the room.

Planning Makes Perfect

It takes more than a little planning to make a stencil look as though it was designed just for your space. The basic rules for planning out your stencil pattern are the same no matter what surface you stencil on.

1. Begin by deciding where you want to stencil. You might want a border in your room, but do you want it at the top of the wall, above the baseboard, or at chair-rail height? Or, you may have the perfect vase on which to stencil, but should you run the stencil vertically or horizontally on that vase? Whatever you decide, make sure you have a basic idea of what you want the finished product to look like before you continue. It's a good idea to draw the design out on a piece of paper first to test different looks.

2. Measure the space where the stencil will go. Then, measure the length of the stencil design, also called a repeat. How many repeats of the design will fit in your space? To find out, divide the length of the space by the length of

If a design does not fit a certain space perfectly, repeat parts of the stencil to help fill the space.

the design. Don't be discouraged by the math; this is easier than it sounds. For example: The wall is 60 inches wide, the stencil repeat is 12 inches. Five repeats will fit on the wall. You won't always get a whole number telling you how many repeats will fit, however. Most of the time you'll wind up with a fraction of a repeat. While that's not such a big deal in a large wall border, it will stand out on a small project. Be creative in getting the stencil to work in the space: You can stretch or shrink the design by adding or removing space between repeats.

3. **Before you begin, do a test to make sure everything will fit.** Make samples of your design on a piece of paper, and tape them into position. Step back and judge the scale of the stencil for the space. Then check to see how adding or removing space between repeats affects the look of the design. Once you're happy with the way the design is planned out, you're ready to paint!

Problem areas

Unfortunately, not every area to be stenciled is a straight, smooth expanse. The space might suddenly become narrower than the stencil, the repeat of the design may fall in a corner, or the surface may be curved, preventing you from stenciling in a straight line.

Ceilings. The ceiling of a room is just like a fifth wall and may be stenciled in the same way. Spray adhesive is a good idea for this

surface because without it gravity will cause the center of the stencil to sag down.

Narrowing space. The best way to deal with a narrowing space is to stop the design and restart where the space returns to the normal width. Fill in the narrow space with elements from the original stencil or with a coordinating, but narrower, stencil.

Corners. Both outside and inside corners can be tricky. Even if you try to plan the space so the repeats don't fall in corners, continuous-line stencils, like vines, might have to go through, inside, or around a corner.

For an outside corner, adhere the stencil and work toward the corner, with the excess stencil extending past the corner. Once you've finished with the first side, carefully fold the stencil around the corner, releasing the first side as you tape down the second. Then continue with the rest of the design.

Inside corners are tougher but not impossible. First, mask off the adjoining wall with a strip of vertical tape. Then, much as with outside corners, tape the stencil down and work the first wall, painting into the corner with the rest of the stencil hanging free. Use less paint, a gentle touch, and don't worry if the image doesn't get completely filled in. Then move the stencil to the second wall, leaving the first side loose while you finish stenciling. You can go back later with an artist's brush to fill in details if you like. As long as you don't smear the image or leave globs of paint, admirers will be fooled into thinking the corner is perfect.

Curved surface. It's hard to keep a straight line when the stencil won't lay flat on a curved surface. Work the stencil in small sections, readjusting every few inches to keep the image on your guideline. This will provide the illusion of a straight line.

Stenciling an outside corner: Wrap the stencil around the corner, releasing the first side as you tape down the second.

For an inside corner, mask off the second wall and let that part of the stencil hang free while you work the first wall.

Let's Paint!

While stenciling is not difficult, it does require knowledge of a few basic techniques. It's a good idea to take the time to practice the techniques listed here on a piece of poster board or cardboard before painting on the real surface. This is also the time to test the colors you've chosen and experiment with highlighting or shading. Once you're confident in your growing skills, move on to your project.

Getting ready

The first step in any painting project is to make sure the surface is properly prepared. Generally, this means that it is clean, dry, and in good repair, but some surfaces, such as metal or plastic, may require special preparation. In addition, before you pour that first drop of paint:

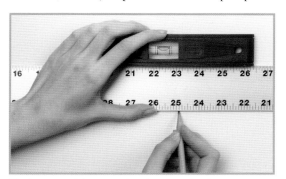

Marking guidelines with a level and ruler

• **Mark guidelines to help keep the design level on the wall or the same distance from the edge of the table.** You can't always count on the ceiling or the edge of the stencil to be your guide. They may look straight, but they often aren't! Place a level on the wall to make sure your guidelines are straight, and make a light pencil mark or run a strip of tape to mark the guideline.

• **Pick a starting point.** On a wall, this should be the most inconspicuous place unless you've carefully calculated whole repeats. With accessory projects, you might start on the back of the piece or maybe in the center so the ends come out the same on both sides.

• **Adhere the stencil to the location of the first repeat using either stencil adhesive or tape.** Mark the registration points if you're using a multiple-overlay stencil.

• **If you have a single-overlay stencil with multiple colors, mask off nearby areas you don't plan to paint yet.** Either tape over the open spaces or hold an index card to mask as you paint. This will keep colors from straying.

• **Prepare your palette.** Pour just a small amount of each color, leaving plenty of room between colors so they don't run into each other. If using crème pots, follow the directions on the pots to remove the skin and reveal the paint.

Choosing colors

Different colors can make a design look entirely different. A soft, dusky rose and Wedgwood blue may bring a calm, country feel to a design, while lime green and purple will make it eclectic and funky. Make sure your color choice achieves the effect you're seeking before you begin painting.

Loading the brush

Proper loading of paint is crucial to a successful project. Too much paint on the brush causes paint to seep under the stencil, ruining your work. It's always better to start light and build up the color.

To get just the right amount of paint on the brush, dip the flat tip into the paint, then swirl the brush on a paper towel to remove most of it. The brush should feel dry to the touch and shouldn't leave paint if you gently touch your hand with it. If it feels wet, swirl it on the paper towel again to remove more paint.

Applying paint

There are two basic techniques you can use with a stencil brush. Each gives a slightly different look, and you might find one easier to do than the other.

Stippling. Hold the brush perpendicular to the surface, and tap up and down with the brush to apply color. The effect is that of lots of little dots created by the bristles of the brush. With stippling, the stencil is less likely to move around so you're less likely to get paint under the edges. However, when working on a large project, it can get tiring.

Swirling. This technique is generally used with stencil crèmes, not acrylics. To create a smooth finish, hold the brush perpendicular to the surface, letting it rest just on the surface, and swirl it in small circles to color in the area. Take care not to push the paint under the edges of the stencil. With swirling, there will be some buildup of paint around the edges.

Adding shading

For either of the two methods, when working with just one color, start on the outside edges of the opening and work into the center. This creates a dark, shadowed edge and light, highlighted center, adding depth to the piece without additional colors. Darken the color by applying more pressure to the brush, not more paint.

To stipple paint, hold the brush perpendicular to the surface and tap up and down repeatedly.

To swirl paint, let the brush rest on the surface and swirl it around in a circular motion.

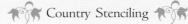

Shading with a darker color

When using more than one color, start with the lightest color first to fill in the space and create the highlight. Then use a darker color worked from the outside edge in to the center. You can then dry-brush a darker color to create a shadow effect on the very edges. For realistic shading, a light touch and little paint are needed.

Moving on

When you've finished the design, carefully remove the stencil from the surface to avoid smudging any wet paint. Move the stencil over, line it up with your guidelines, and re-adhere to start the next image.

When working with multiple-overlay stencils, it's a good idea to work the entire area with the first overlay, then go back with the next layer, and then the next. This allows the paint to dry before the next stencil goes over it, eliminating the risk of smudges. Acrylic paints, however, often dry quickly enough that it's possible to complete the entire image at one time before moving on to the next repeat.

Overlapping components

When part of a design seems to "disappear" behind another part, always stencil the object in front first. This keeps ghost images and paint ridges from being visible underneath. After stenciling the first object, cover it with the dropout piece from your stencil and tape in place. This allows you to stencil images "behind" the already-stenciled object without worrying about paint drips or overlap ridges.

Cleaning up

Take some time to step back and admire your artistic endeavor, but the work isn't quite over yet! Proper cleanup will keep your materials in good shape for your next stenciling project.

To preserve the life of brushes and stencils, clean them thoroughly after every use. Acrylic paints clean up with soap and water, whereas oil paints need mineral spirits or brush cleaner. Oil soap, which is formulated for use on wood, is great for cleaning brushes because it won't dry them out. Some plastic stencils just require a soaking in water to remove acrylic paint; others need to be scrubbed gently. Try an all-purpose cleaner, using a toothbrush or sponge very gently for any scrubbing. Mineral spirits remove adhesive from the backs of stencils.

Trick of the Trade: Because the bridges of stencils can be quite delicate, use a soft touch when scrubbing.

Protecting your work

While it's not always necessary to seal your work with a protective coat, a clear coat will keep your work fresh for a long time—especially if it's in a high traffic area or if it will be handled frequently. Clear coats range from matte to gloss; decide how shiny you want the surface to be. Keep in mind that the clear coat will change the color and appearance of the surface slightly, so apply it to the entire surface, not just the stenciled area.

Trick of the Trade: Furniture, floorcloths, and floors need extra protection, so several coats of sealer are necessary on those areas.

Make Your Own Stencils

Sometimes you just can't find the stencil you want, or the perfect design is not scaled right for your space. Now what? You don't have to settle for something that's not exactly right. It's not difficult to make your own stencils!

Almost any kind of clear plastic will make a good stencil because it won't absorb paint and you can see through it to trace the design. The thinner the plastic, the more careful you need to be when cutting out the design, stenciling, and cleaning the template. Buy blank sheets of Mylar at a craft and hobby store; also check the quilting section for large sheets of template plastic. You can also use overhead acetate or X-ray film for making templates.

Another option, though not as durable as plastic, is paper. Cardstock and poster board are rigid and strong enough for accurate stenciling but not flexible enough for bending at corners. You can also treat just about any thick paper with linseed oil to make it waterproof.

Designing the stencil

Sketch, trace, or computer-draft your design, then use a photocopier to make it the right size.

Decide if this design works best as a single- or multiple-overlay stencil. With a single overlay, you'll have to plan for bridges between major areas of the stencil to make the shapes distinct. For example, a pear would require bridges between the pear and the stem and between the stem and the leaf. The more complicated the image, the more bridges you will need.

Go with multiple overlays for a more realistic finish or if the image is quite detailed. Place a piece of tracing paper over the image, and trace all the parts to be cut out. Then number all the areas for the first overlay with a 1, keeping in mind that images on the same overlay cannot touch each other. Number areas for the next overlay with a 2, and so on until all the areas have been numbered. This tells you how many overlays you will need. Be sure to include dots in the corners for registration points so you will be able to line up the multiple overlays later.

Making the stencil

If using a transparent material, lay your design underneath and trace it onto the blank with a permanent marker. Tape the copy and your blank down. For opaque blanks, place carbon paper between the design and the blank, with the carbon side on the blank and the design on top, then trace the lines. Leave at least an inch of blank material around the outside of the design.

To cut the stencil, you'll need a sharp craft knife or an electric stencil cutter, which makes quick work of cutting plastic blanks. Work on a surface that won't be damaged by the knife or the heat of the cutter; a sheet of glass is ideal.

Try to cut in one continuous line; the piece should just fall out when you're done. If it's still hanging on, take your blade back through the line to get a smooth edge; don't try to pull it, or you'll get a ragged edge. It will take some practice, so don't be discouraged if your first efforts don't look like a commercial stencil.

Test out your practice designs to see how closely they create the image you want. When you're satisfied, go ahead and start stenciling!

Miscellaneous tips

Repair. Stencils sometimes tear, but repairs are easily made. For plastic stencils, you'll need transparent tape and a craft knife. For paper stencils, use masking tape and a craft knife. Tape the top and bottom of the damaged areas, sticky sides together, then cut away the excess tape.

Storage. Stencils should be stored flat. Underbed boxes and dresser drawers are good places for flat storage; you can hang large stencils on pants hangers in a closet. Don't roll or bend a stencil in any way, or it won't lay flat the next time you want to use it.

Making your own stencil on a transparent material

When making your own stencil, try to cut in one fluid line to achieve a smooth edge.

To repair a paper stencil, use masking tape and a craft knife.

Using This Book

The projects in this book include a wide variety of styles and techniques. Take a moment to look through the pages. Get inspired by the beautiful country colors and designs! You'll find everything from traditional country floral faux wallpaper to romantic French country tiles to a rustic moose lampshade. Each project features complete step-by-step instructions and photos to help make everything easy to understand. Each project is also rated for difficulty and indicates the amount of time needed to complete it. (Of course, the time varies based on the size of the room and your experience level.)

Follow the tips found in this introduction as well as the specific instructions for each project to create glorious country stencils throughout your home. We recommend that the first time you try a particular design, you follow the directions exactly. Then, when you have perfected it, go ahead and experiment all you want! Using the designs as a starting point for colors and layout, vary them to match your color scheme and tastes. You may want to use one or more of the many suggestions for design variations for each project!

Stencils for all the projects featured in these pages are found in the back of this book. After using a stencil and cleaning it, tuck it into the handy pocket to store it for future use.

Happy stenciling!

Seed-Packet
Pots

*Enliven ordinary clay pots with these nostalgic
seed-packet designs. Indoors or out, your vegetable
garden never looked so appealing.*

WHAT YOU'LL NEED

- Heavyweight paper
- Scissors
- Terra cotta or clay pots, 3
- Delta Ceramcoat acrylic paint: White, Ivory, Adobe, Tomato Spice, Poppy Orange, Dark Burnt Umber
- Americana acrylic paint: Hauser Medium Green, Hauser Dark Green
- Accent acrylic paint: Raw Umber
- Folk Art acrylic paint: Bright Pink
- 1-inch stencil brushes, 3
- ⅝-inch stencil brushes, 2
- ⅜-inch stencil brushes, 7

Stencils for this project are located on page 89.

1 Cut a 4×3-inch rectangle out of heavyweight paper. This will be your template for the blank seed packet.

2 Center this paper rectangle vertically on the clay pot, and trace around it with a pencil.

Step 2

Remove the paper. Affix low-adhesive tape around the outer edges of the penciled rectangle, leaving a 4×3-inch open space.

3 Using a 1-inch stencil brush, basecoat the rectangle White. Let dry. Repeat.

4 With the tape still in place, pounce Ivory around the edge of the rectangle with a 1-inch brush. Fade this color into the center, leaving the center area white. Let dry.

5 Stencil each seed packet as follows, using a ⅜-inch brush unless otherwise indicated.

Tomato: Position and tape down the large tomato stencil. Stencil the tomato Adobe with a ⅝-inch brush, concentrating the color on the edges and leaving the center light. Shade around the edges with Tomato Spice. Fill in the lettering with Raw Umber.

Step 4

Position and tape down the tomato overlay. Stencil the leaves Hauser Medium Green, and shade with Hauser Dark Green.

Carrot: Position and tape down the carrot stencil. Basecoat the carrot Poppy Orange. Shade around the edges with Hauser Dark Green. Stencil the leaf Hauser Dark Green. Stencil the letters Raw Umber.

Position and tape down the carrot overlay. Basecoat the leaves Hauser Medium Green, and shade with Hauser Dark Green. Stencil the carrot's detail lines Hauser Dark Green.

Radish: Position and tape down the radish stencil. Basecoat the radish Bright Pink. Shade around the edges with Tomato Spice, fading into the center and leaving a highlight. Stencil the leaves Hauser Medium Green.

Step 5

Position and tape down the radish overlay. Stencil the leaf detail Hauser Dark Green and the letters Raw Umber.

6 At each corner of the seed packet, measure in ⅝ inch both horizontally and vertically along the taped edges. Make a pencil mark on the tape (not on the pot itself) at these measurements. Connect the pencil marks at each corner with a piece of tape placed toward the inside of the seed packet. Stencil these taped-off areas Hauser Medium Green, and add shading around the edges of the triangles with Hauser Dark Green. Let dry, then remove the diagonal pieces of tape.

7 Shade around the edges of the entire seed packet in Dark Burnt Umber with a 1-inch brush. Let dry. Carefully remove the tape from the pot.

8 Center the border stencil vertically on the rim of the pot. Tape in place. Stencil the leaves Hauser Medium Green, and shade

Step 6

with Hauser Dark Green. Use a ⅝-inch brush to stencil the border flowers: On the carrot pot, use Poppy Orange; on the tomato and radish pots, use Tomato Spice. Repeat around the rim.

Seed-Packet Pots
Variations

Uncomplicated, simple designs are perfect for sharpening your stenciling skills. Practice on heavy paper first, using multiple colors and shadings to produce more realistic vegetables. Designs like these are especially versatile—try them out on household accessories such as kitchen canisters, backsplash tiles, or pantry doors. However you use them, they'll make quite a statement!

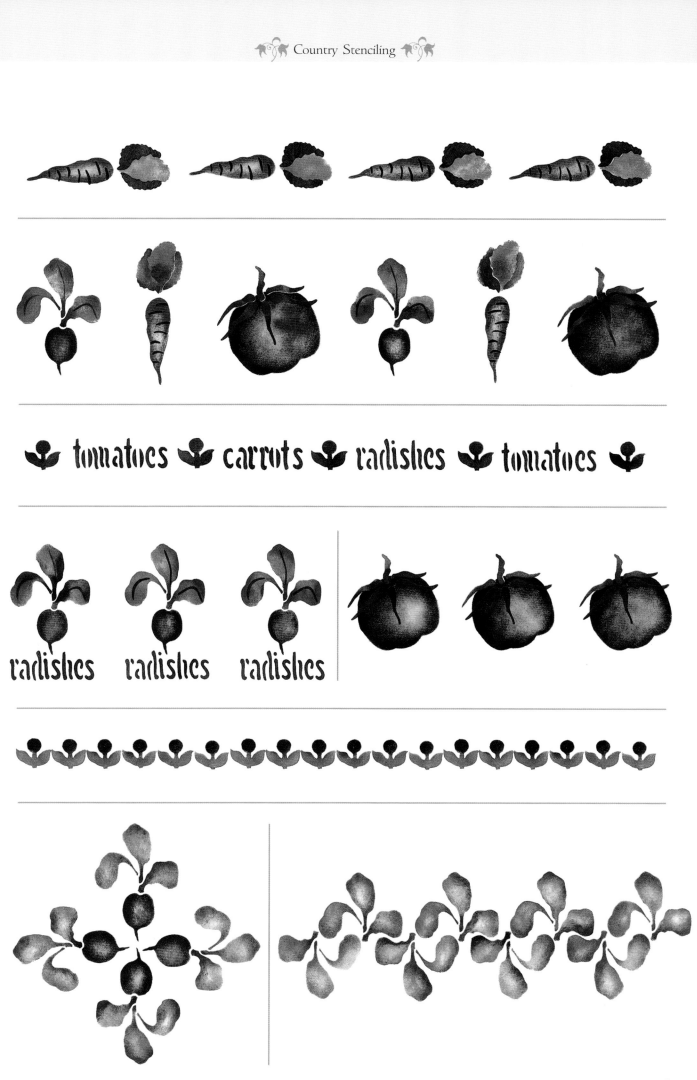

tomatoes ❦ carrots ❦ radishes ❦ tomatoes ❦

radishes   radishes   radishes

Farmhouse
Plate & Shelf

*Fool-the-eye stenciling works its delightful magic
here to create a faux plate. The supporting shelf is real,
but its matching design accents the plate nicely.*

Trick of the Trade: For a lovely touch, apply a sponged- or rag-finish texture to the wall beneath the stencil.

WHAT YOU'LL NEED

- Delta Ceramcoat acrylic paint: Light Ivory, Dark Burnt Umber, Black Green, Poppy Orange, Tomato Spice
- Americana acrylic paint: Hauser Medium Green
- 1¼-inch stencil brush
- ⅝-inch stencil brush
- ⅜-inch stencil brushes, 4

Stencils for this project are located on pages 91 and 93.

 To prepare the wall for the faux plate stencil, basecoat with latex paint. Determine where the plate will be painted on the wall, then measure and mark a vertical line where the center of the plate will be. Use a plumb line or level to make sure the line is straight.

 The plate stencil provided is only half the image. Line up the stencil along either side of the guideline, and tape it in place.

3 Basecoat this half of the plate Light Ivory with the 1¼-inch brush. Let dry, and repeat if necessary.

4 Dry the stencil completely, then flip it over and line it up with the first half of the image. Tape it in place and repeat step 3. Touch up the center area, where the 2 sides come together. Let paint dry.

5 Leaving the stencil in place, shade around the outer edge of the plate with Dark Burnt Umber. Dry the stencil, and reposition on the other side. Shade again with Dark Burnt Umber.

6 To find the center of the plate, measure and make a small pencil mark in the middle. Align the center plate stencil with this mark, and tape it in place. Shade just the edge of this inner section with Dark Burnt Umber. Dry the stencil, then reposition it on the other side of the plate and repeat.

7 Center the fruit design stencil on the plate, and tape in place. Basecoat the leaves and stems Hauser Medium Green, and shade them with Black Green. Stencil the fruits and berries Poppy Orange with the ⅝-inch brush. Shade the edges of the fruits and berries Tomato Spice.

Step 2

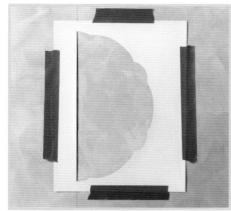

Step 5

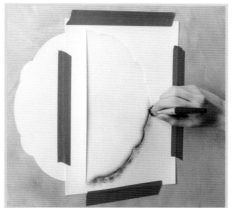

Step 6

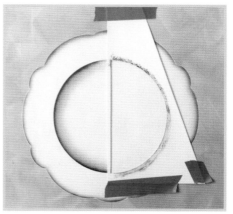

Farmhouse Plate & Shelf
Variations

Create a collection of stenciled plates by varying the central designs for a set of faux dishes. Stencil them as a border above kitchen cabinets or on a tabletop itself for a whimsical touch. Adjust the size of the plate stencil to create luncheon plates or larger platters. But why stop there? Stencil designs that complement your personal style on purchased tableware or china for one-of-a-kind table settings.

Flowers & Ivy
Nook

Winding ivy and sprigs of wildflowers accent this inviting nook, transforming it into a welcoming, comfortable retreat.

WHAT YOU'LL NEED

- Scrap paper
- Scissors
- Ruler and level
- Delta Ceramcoat acrylic paint: Wedgwood Green, Dusty Plum, Dusty Purple, Blue Wisp, Avalon Blue
- Americana acrylic paint: Hauser Dark Green
- ⅝-inch stencil brush
- ⅜-inch stencil brushes, 5

Stencils for this project are located on page 95.

1 To prepare the wall, basecoat with latex paint. Before stenciling the flowers onto the wall, first trace all the patterns onto a sheet of paper and photocopy them. Make as many copies as you think you will need (the number of flowers you intend to stencil onto the wall). Cut out each design (you don't have to be too meticulous—a rough outline will do the job). Plan your layout by taping the copies to the wall. Turn the patterns in various directions to avoid a repetitive look, and move them around on the wall until you're happy with the design. Leave at least 6½

inches empty along the bottom for the border.

2 Working on 1 flower at a time, hold each stencil over its paper copy. Tape 1 edge of the stencil in place, and remove the copy. Secure the other edge of the stencil.

3 Stencil the designs as follows:

Small Ivy Sprig: Basecoat the ivy Wedgwood Green with a ⅝-inch brush, and shade some of the edges with Hauser Dark Green. Also use Hauser Dark Green for the stems.

Five-Petal Flowers: Stencil the leaves Wedgwood Green using the ⅝-inch brush, and use Hauser Dark Green to shade some of the edges. Stencil the stems Hauser

Step 2

Dark Green. Basecoat 2 of the flowers Dusty Plum, and shade them with Dusty Purple. Base the third flower Blue Wisp, using Avalon Blue for shading.

Small Flower Curl: Stencil the stems and leaves as you did for the Five-Petal Flowers. Basecoat the flowers Blue Wisp, and shade them with Avalon Blue.

4 To create the border, use a pencil and ruler to measure and mark a line 6½ inches up from the floor or molding. Mask the upper edge with low-adhesive tape. Paint this border a shade darker than the rest of the wall. Let dry, and leave the tape in place.

5 Create the border's 2 stripes by placing a strip of tape ¼ inch below the upper edge of the border and another strip ⅜ inch above the molding. Paint the stripes Dusty Purple. Let dry, and remove the tape.

6 Use a level and pencil to measure and mark a faint pencil line horizontally through the center of the border. This will

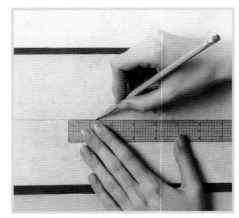

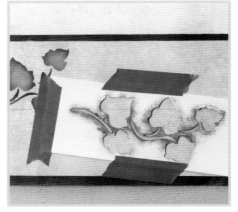

Step 6

provide a guideline for the ivy placement.

Position the stem of ivy stencil A at the beginning of the pencil line, and angle the leaves upward so the top leaf is

Step 7

about ¼ inch from the top stripe. Stencil this ivy as you did the ivy in step 3. Remove the stencil.

At the end of stencil A, position ivy stencil B on the pencil line. Angle the leaves

Step 8

down this time, with the bottom leaf in this group about ¼ inch from the bottom stripe. Remove the stencil.

Repeat steps 7 and 8 until the border is complete.

Flowers & Ivy Nook
Variations

Design your own custom wallpaper and border with this stencil combination. Or consider this pattern for built-in shelves, a pantry, or a small hallway. For a brighter palette, work the stencils in cheerful spring shades. Extend the charm by stenciling a flower or two onto a mirror, throw pillow, or coordinating floorcloth.

Barnyard Animals Chair

*What child wouldn't welcome the opportunity to
read a book or tell a story while perched on this charming
little chair? It's a treasure they'll save forever.*

WHAT YOU'LL NEED

- Child-size wooden chair
- Sandpaper
- Wood sealer
- Index cards
- Delta Ceramcoat acrylic paint: Light Ivory, Light Foliage Green, Mello Yellow, Crocus Yellow, Tomato Spice, Cape Cod Blue
- Delta Stencil Paint Crème: Garden Green, Cottage Blue, Basic Black, Sunflower Yellow, Yellow Ochre, Warm Brown
- 1-inch flat brushes, 2
- ½-inch stencil brushes, 6
- ¼-inch stencil brushes, 2
- Toothpick
- Satin-finish spray varnish
- Satin-finish brush-on varnish

Stencils for this project are located on page 97.

1. Prepare the wood for painting by lightly sanding it with fine-grade sandpaper, applying a wood sealer, and basecoating as follows: Paint seat, seat apron, and backrest slats Light Ivory; top edges of backrest slats and 1-inch squares on front corners of seat Light Foliage Green; front of vertical rails and 1-inch stripe around seat 1 coat Mello Yellow followed by a thin coat of Crocus Yellow; rungs of legs and ¼-inch stripe on front edge of seat Tomato Spice; and chair legs Cape Cod Blue. Let dry.

2. To make the seat border, tape the checkerboard stencil to the edge of the seat. Using Tomato Spice and a ¼-inch brush, stencil the first row of checks along the edge of the seat. Lift the stencil and move it 1 row to the right and 1 row in to stencil the inside row of checks. Be sure the corners of the checks touch. Repeat around the entire seat border, except for the green corner squares.

3. To add a stripe between the checkerboard border and the seat, tape 2 index cards together, ⅛ inch apart. The space between them will be the stripe. Position the stripe so it touches the edge of the checkerboard border. Tape in place, and stencil the stripe Light Foliage Green. Repeat around the seat so the entire checkerboard is edged in green.

4. Tape the chicken wire stencil to the small backrest slat, and swirl Garden Green into the openings of the stencil. Move the stencil over, and repeat until the chicken wire covers the backrest slat, front and back. Repeat on the seat apron.

5. Tape the cow stencil onto the seat, and mark the registration points. Basecoat the cow Cottage Blue using a ½-inch brush, and shade with Basic Black. Stencil the horns, tail hair, and hooves Basic Black. Stencil the bow on the cow's tail Tomato Spice. Remove the stencil.

6. Position the cow overlay, and tape it in place. Stencil

Step 2

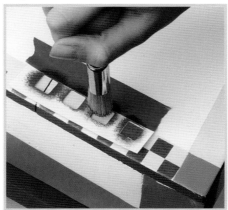

Step 3

the nostrils, eyes, and body markings Basic Black. Let dry.

7 Tape chick stencil C to the left corner of the seat. Using a ½-inch brush, stencil the chick Sunflower Yellow. Add shading with Yellow Ochre, and stencil the chick's feet and beak Warm Brown. Use a toothpick and Basic Black to add a small dot for the chick's eye.

8 Repeat step 7 to stencil chick B in the seat's right corner.

9 Before stenciling the chicks' tracks onto the seat, use a pencil to mark where they will

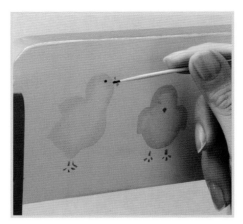

Step 10

go. Once you're happy with the placement, tape down the stencil and stencil the tracks Basic Black with a ¼-inch brush.

10 To stencil the top slat on the backrest, follow the instructions in step 7 to stencil 3 chicks onto the backrest,

referring to the photo for placement. Use the face overlay for the middle chick, and stencil the beak Warm Brown and the eyes Basic Black. Mask off the chick on the left, then stencil a checkerboard border around the slat (see step 2). Repeat the design on the back of the slat.

11 Mist the entire surface of the chair with at least 2 coats of spray varnish, letting it dry between coats. Let this dry several days, and then brush on 2 smooth coats of varnish for more protection from the hands and feet of little ones.

Barnyard Animals Chair
Variations

Count your chicks—they're likely to hatch everywhere once you begin this easy design! Change the color of the checkerboard to coordinate with your décor, and stencil a fun wraparound border. Mix and match your favorite barnyard elements to enliven different areas of the playroom for a down-on-the-farm look.

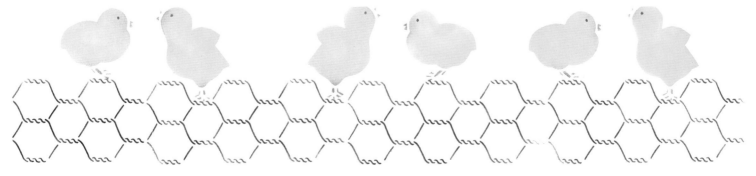

Bountiful
Fruit Buckets

Farmstand charm brings these
beautiful buckets to life. What a lovely addition
to a kitchen or pantry!

Trick of the Trade: To achieve a realistic three-dimensional effect, apply color more intensely around the edges of the fruit and leaves and keep the centers lighter.

WHAT YOU'LL NEED

- Galvanized metal bucket
- Dishwashing detergent
- Fine-grade sandpaper
- Metal primer
- 1-inch foam brush
- ½-inch stencil brushes, 7
- Gel blending medium
- Delta Ceramcoat acrylic paint: Apple Green, Tomato Spice, Light Ivory, Calypso Orange, Grape, Medium Foliage Green, Dark Foliage Green, Brown Iron Oxide
- Toothpick
- Satin-finish spray varnish

Stencils for this project are located on page 97.

1 To prepare the bucket for painting, wash it with detergent or a household cleaner. Let dry. Lightly sand the surface with fine-grade sandpaper. Apply an even coat of metal primer with a foam brush, and let dry.

2 Basecoat the bucket Apple Green. Let dry, and repeat.

3 Use spray adhesive to adhere the checkerboard stencil to the top rim of the bucket. Swirl Tomato Spice into the squares, then move the stencil over and repeat the squares all the way around the top. Let dry. Now position the stencil so that the red squares are covered, and stencil the remaining spaces Light Ivory. Repeat to finish the border.

4 Repeat step 3 to create a checkerboard at the bottom of the bucket.

5 Use spray adhesive to adhere the apple stencil to the front of the bucket, centering the bottom of the image between the 2 handles. Basecoat the apple Calypso Orange. Let dry, and then apply Tomato Spice around the perimeter of the apple. The red will be just an outline of color at this point.

6 Before extending red into the center of the apple, flip the dropout of the apple upside down and position it on the bucket so the top curve of the apple covers the section that will become the stem cavity. Hold the dropout in place rather than taping it down. Continue swirling Tomato Spice around the apple and along the bottom edge of the dropout, keeping the center of the apple quite light. Remove the dropout and work the paint onto the top edge of the apple, leaving a strong Calypso Orange highlight to create the stem cavity. Blend the color along the edges. Let dry.

7 Cover the apple with its dropout to protect it while you stencil the grapes. Basecoat the grapes Calypso Orange. Let dry, then swirl Grape paint onto the entire cluster of grapes. Don't worry at this point about making each individual grape distinct. Repeat with a second coat of

Step 5

Step 6

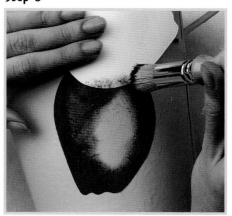

Grape. It's OK if some of the orange shows through.

Using the brush that already has Grape on it, pick up a little Light Ivory from your palette. Hold the individual grape stencil in place, and touch highlights onto the right side and around the bottom of each individual grape. Don't strive to make each grape exactly the same; subtle differences and nuances add interest. Using a toothpick, dot Light Ivory highlights on the right side of each grape. Finally, load Medium Foliage Green on the same brush, and lightly add shading between the grapes and the apple.

9 With the apple dropout still in place, position the leaf stencil and basecoat the leaf

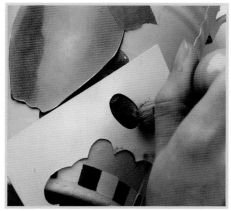

Step 8

Calypso Orange. Let dry, then swirl Medium Foliage Green onto the leaf. Shade with Dark Foliage Green near the apple, and add a very thin coat of Tomato Spice over the darkest areas of the leaf. Repeat for the second leaf.

10 Position the pear stencil over the top of the apple dropout, and basecoat the pear Calypso Orange. Let dry, then brush a very soft blush of Tomato Spice, blending it softly into the basecoat. Repeat with Medium

Step 11

Foliage Green to add a tint of green behind the leaves. Remove the apple dropout.

11 Position the stem stencil so it fits into the stem cavity highlight on the apple, and adhere. Stencil the stem Brown Iron Oxide. Flip the stencil over, adhere it to the top of the pear, and repeat.

12 To protect the bucket, spray the surface with at least 2 coats of varnish. Let dry between coats.

Bountiful Fruit Buckets
Variations

This project is the perfect place to experiment with color and shading. Try a monochromatic color scheme for a subtle look, or turn that red delicious apple into a golden delicious treat. Perch the apples on a checkerboard rail, or make them the focal point of a tile. Repeat a few clusters of fabulously rich grapes and leaves for a room border, or isolate any element for a canvas market bag. Then sit back, and enjoy the fruits of your labor.

French
Country Kitchen

*Behind the warmth of a French country kitchen
lies a brilliant surprise…the blue tiles, as well as the
dramatic swag, are faux treatments!*

WHAT YOU'LL NEED

- Delta Ceramcoat acrylic paint: Periwinkle Blue, White, Light Ivory, Dark Burnt Umber
- Folk Art acrylic paint: Blue Ink
- ⅝-inch stencil brushes, 2
- ⅜-inch stencil brushes, 2
- 1-inch stencil brush
- Heavy paper or cardstock
- Craft knife

Stencils for this project are located on page 99.

Trick of the Trade:
For an extra-special look, install decorative wood molding to help define your faux tiles. In our photo, we added ¼-inch molding to the top and to the bottom.

FLORAL SWAG

1 Determine where the swag will be painted on the wall, then measure and mark a vertical line where the center will be. Use a plumb line or level to make sure the line is straight.

2 The swag stencil provided is only half the image. Line up the stencil along 1 side of the guideline, and tape it in place.

3 Basecoat the entire stencil in Periwinkle Blue with a ⅝-inch brush, then shade with Blue Ink using a ⅜-inch brush. Let dry.

4 Flip the stencil over and line it up with the first half of the image. Tape the stencil in place, masking your previous work on the center edge. Repeat step 3.

FAUX TILES

1 To create a tile stencil, measure and mark a 4×4-inch square on heavy paper or cardstock, leaving at least 1 inch as a border around all 4 edges. Cut out the square with a craft knife.

2 Position the homemade tile stencil on the wall just above the countertop. Basecoat the tile

White with a 1-inch brush, then shade around the tile's edges with Light Ivory on a ⅝-inch brush, brushing in about ½ inch on all 4 sides. Let dry completely, and remove the stencil.

3 Position the floral design stencil on the tile, and tape it in place. Basecoat the design Periwinkle Blue with a ⅝-inch brush, and use a ⅜-inch brush to

Step 3—Floral Swag

Step 4—Floral Swag

Step 1—Faux Tiles

Step 3—Faux Tiles

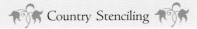
shade the "insides" of the flowers with Blue Ink (see photo for the detail). Let dry.

4 Reposition and tape down the square tile stencil. For a dimensional effect, lightly shade just the edges of the tile with Dark Burnt Umber using a ⅜-inch brush, shading over the blue flower petals in the corners.

5 Reposition the tile stencil ⅛ inch from the first tile. This will create the illusion of a grout line.

6 Repeat steps 2–5 for each faux tile.

Step 4—Faux Tiles

French Country Kitchen
Variations

Make this elegant swag the focal point of any room! Add flourishes and flowers to further embellish the design, or subtract any of the elements for a more restrained look. With a simple change of color, you have a brand-new swag. Adding faux tiles is a stylish way to dress up a room. Vary the look by dropping out some of the center designs, using different patterns and colors, or changing the color of the background grout.

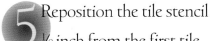

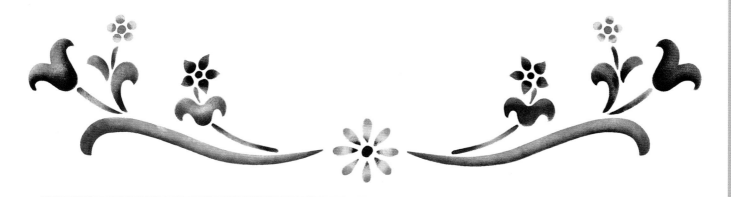

Garden Butterfly
Border

*These graceful blue and yellow
butterflies inspire imagination and whimsy
in any room of the house.*

WHAT YOU'LL NEED

- Delta Stencil Paint Crème: Amber, Bark Brown, Colonial Green, Paprika, Basic Black, Goldenrod, Cottage Blue, Garnet Red
- ½-inch stencil brushes, 4
- ¼-inch stencil brushes, 3

Stencils for this project are located on page 101.

1 Use a pencil, ruler, and level or plumb line to indicate where the border will be stenciled. Make sure the lines are parallel to the mirror frame.

2 Center the grapevine stencil on the pencil line, and tape it in place. Stencil the vine Amber using a ½-inch brush, then add Bark Brown shading with a ¼-inch brush anywhere a twig disappears behind another. Repeat all the way around the pencil line.

Step 4

3 Working in groups of 3, indicate the placement of leaves around the grapevine. Use the 3 different leaf shapes, and vary the placement so as not to create a pattern.

4 Position and adhere the leaf stencils 1 at a time. Mark the registration points. Use a ½-inch brush to stencil the leaves Colonial Green, making them darker at the stem and around the edges. With a ¼-inch brush, add tints of Paprika. Next, use a ¼-inch brush to subtly shade

Step 2

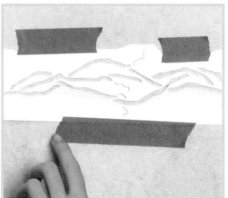

Step 5

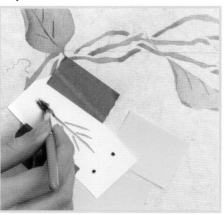

with Basic Black. Let the colors blend gently, and avoid making each leaf exactly alike.

5 For each leaf, align the registration marks of the second overlay, and tape it down. Stencil each leaf detail Colonial Green, and shade with a tiny bit of Basic Black.

6 Position the butterflies between the leaves, balancing the blue and yellow. Make a light pencil mark to indicate placement.

7 Adhere the small butterfly stencil to the wall where indicated, and mark the registration points. Stencil this butterfly Goldenrod, then remove the overlay and wipe clean. Position the second overlay, and stencil the wing detail Amber. Stencil the body and

Step 7

antennae Basic Black. Repeat for all of the small butterflies.

8 For all of the large butterflies, use Cottage Blue and a ½-inch brush on the first overlay.

Mark the registration points before removing the stencil. Then position and tape down the second overlay, and stencil all of the detail Basic Black.

9 Plan where you will stencil the berries. Position and tape down the berries stencil, and apply Garnet Red with a ½-inch brush. Repeat around the vine.

Garden Butterfly Border
Variations

This stencil pattern can be interpreted with as much or as little freeform style as you choose. Fashion a unique vine with just the leaves and berries, and accent it with a single butterfly. Bring a rainbow of color into your room with multiple colors of butterflies. On the back of a chair, across a pillowcase, or along the edge of a shower curtain, let your imagination lead the way.

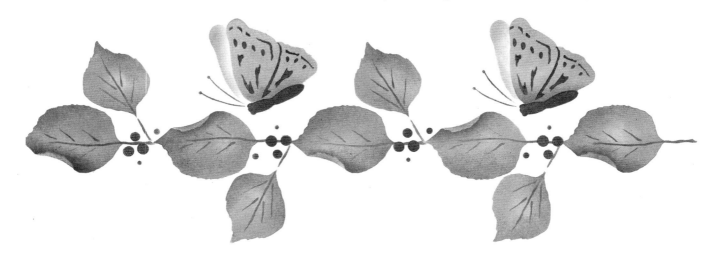

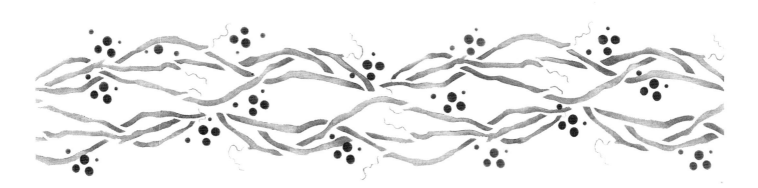

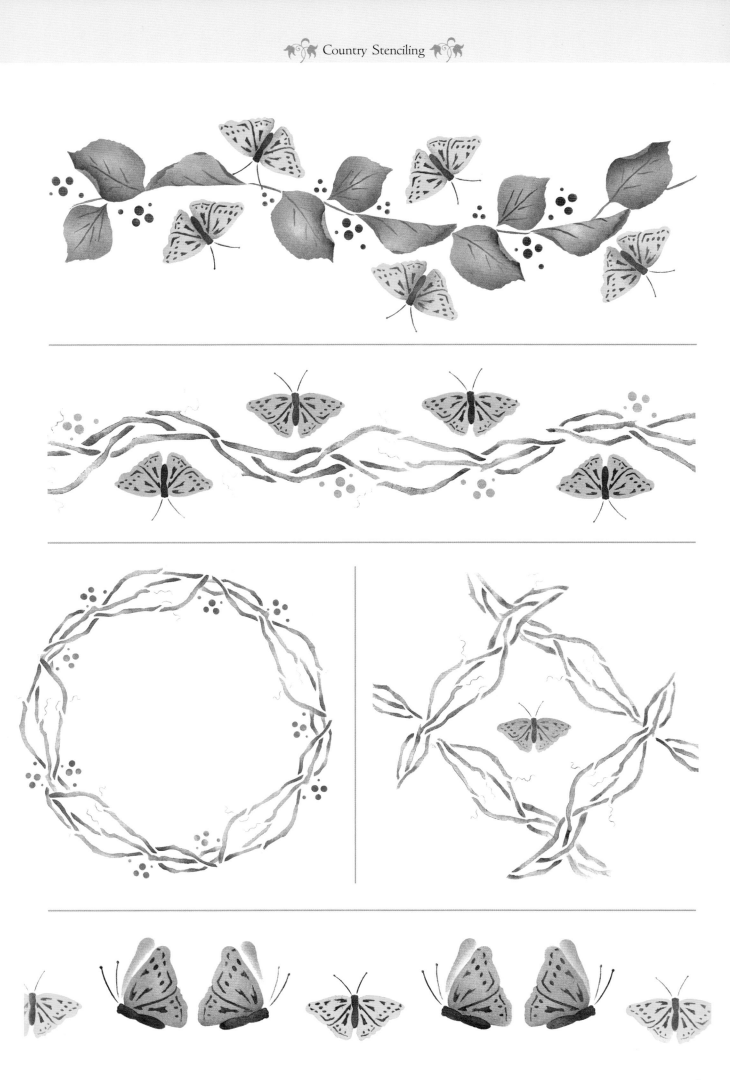

Rustic Moose
Lampshade

This delightful lampshade brings the charm of rustic cabin style home. Its bold, graphic design will light up the room.

WHAT YOU'LL NEED

- Paper lampshade
- Delta Ceramcoat acrylic paint: Brown Iron Oxide
- Folk Art acrylic paint: Licorice
- 1-inch stencil brush
- ⅝-inch stencil brush

Stencils for this project are located on page 103.

1 To create the "ground" along the bottom edge of the lampshade, apply low-adhesive tape all around the bottom edge. Next, apply another piece of tape above the first one in an irregular, bumpy line, leaving about ¼ to 1 inch of space between the 2 strips as you move around the shade. This will give the illusion of slight hills and valleys across the landscape. Press firmly on the edges of the tape to make a seal so paint does not seep underneath.

2 With the 1-inch stencil brush, apply a solid coat of Brown Iron Oxide to the entire ground area. Use the ½-inch stencil brush to shade the top and bottom edges (along the tape lines) with Licorice. Remove the tape, and let dry.

3 Position the moose stencil so the hooves touch the ground. Tape in place. Stencil with Brown Iron Oxide using the 1-inch brush. Shade the edges of the moose with Licorice, using the ⅝-inch brush.

Trick of the Trade: If any parts of the stencil flip up (like the antlers), use your fingers to hold them down while you continue painting.

4 Adhere the moon stencil above the moose. Stencil the moon with Licorice paint using the ⅝-inch brush.

5 Continue the "landscape" by stenciling trees and grass around the shade. Position the stencils along the ground line, and stencil all of the landscaping with Licorice. For visual interest, make the trees different heights by shortening the trunks of some when you place them along the ground line.

Step 1

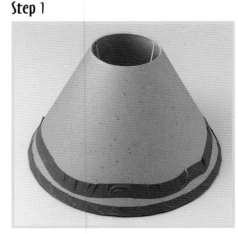

Step 2

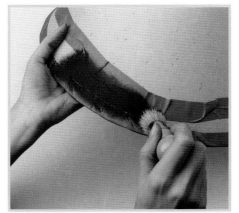

Step 5

Rustic Moose Lampshade
Variations

A single moose makes a strong, graphic statement, and the rust and black shades work well with the wrought-iron base, but why stop there? Change your palette to rich greens and browns for a subtle change. Work the moose and landscape elements together to dress up a fireplace screen, window shades, or even the back of a jean jacket. For a simpler project, consider just the trees and grasses as repeat designs on muslin curtains or throw pillows for a family room.

Welcome Friends
Hallway

The warm colors and heartfelt
sentiment expressed in the border say it all.
Welcome! We're so glad you're here.

WHAT YOU'LL NEED

- Light Ivory latex wall paint
- Delta Ceramcoat acrylic paint: Blueberry, Light Ivory, Antique Gold, Moroccan Red
- Index cards
- ½-inch stencil brush
- ¼-inch stencil brushes, 3

Stencils for this project are located on page 107.

1 Prepare the wall by basecoating with satin- or eggshell-finish Light Ivory latex wall paint.

2 The border is created by taping off and painting stripes of varying widths. To begin, measure and make a light pencil mark before placing the tape. Use a level to make sure the lines are parallel to the floor. Locate the bottom of the border, and mask it off with tape. Measure up ⅛ inch, and mask off this stripe. Paint it Blueberry. Let dry, and remove the tape.

3 Measure up ⅛ inch from the Blueberry stripe (this space remains Light Ivory). Mask off another stripe above the Light Ivory stripe, this one ⅝ inch up. Paint it Antique Gold. Let dry, and remove the tape.

4 Again measure up ⅛ inch (another Light Ivory stripe), and mask off a 7-inch stripe for the center band of the border. Paint this band Blueberry, let dry, and remove the tape.

5 Finish off the border stripes by masking and painting as before, but this time in reverse order: ⅛-inch Light Ivory, ⅝-inch Antique Gold, ⅛-inch Light Ivory, and ⅛-inch Blueberry.

6 To stencil the border, center the words "Welcome Friends" in the Blueberry band, and secure with tape. Stencil the letters Light Ivory. Measure 7 inches from both ends of "Welcome Friends." Reposition the stencil at these points, and paint. Repeat "Welcome Friends" across the entire width of the border.

7 Center the heart motif between the repeats of "Welcome Friends," and tape it in place. Stencil the heart Moroccan Red, the dots Light Ivory, and the leaves Antique Gold using ¼-inch brushes. Repeat across the entire border.

8 Position the dot/leaf design in the Antique Gold stripe. Stencil the dot Moroccan Red and the leaf Blueberry. Repeat across the top and bottom gold stripes.

9 Position the tree 1 inch above the border, centered above the Welcome Friends wording, and tape in place.

Step 2

Step 5

Step 7

Stencil the tree Antique Gold, the heart and apples Moroccan Red, and the leaves Blueberry. Repeat every time "Welcome Friends" is stenciled.

10 For a wallpapered look, stencil the heart motifs on the wall at regular intervals: Measure up 13 inches from the top of every heart motif in the

Step 9

border, and position the heart motif there. Stencil the heart

Moroccan Red, the dots Antique Gold, and the leaves Blueberry. Measure up 10½ inches from the top of the heart above every tree, and repeat the stencil. To add more rows, measure up the same increment from each heart motif, and repeat. Use a level or plum line to make sure the hearts are aligned.

Welcome Friends Hallway
Variations

The variations for this flexible design are endless. Piece together the leaves, the dots, and the hearts in all kinds of different configurations to fit your space. Try stenciling these country icons onto tablecloths, chair backs, pillows, or any other surface that strikes your fancy!

Geranium
Window Shade

Add a splash of color to a workaday room with this design.
Whether tumbling across a roller shade or sprucing up a box,
these geraniums will be a perennial favorite.

WHAT YOU'LL NEED

- Window shade
- Delta Stencil Paint Crème: Garnet Red, Garden Green, Basic Black, Christmas Green, Black Cherry
- ½-inch stencil brushes, 3
- ⅜-inch stencil brushes, 2
- Satin-finish spray varnish

Stencils for this project are located on page 109.

1 Draw a soft pencil line about 6 inches from the bottom of the shade, making sure the line is level. Measure and mark the center of this line to determine where to start stenciling.

2 Position the geranium stencil so that the mark you made is in the center of the round blossom marked "center." Tape in place, and mark the registration points. (Note: The stencil provided is only half the image. After stenciling the first half, you will flip the stencil over and stencil the other half.)

3 Stencil all the flowers Garnet Red with a ½-inch brush, keeping the paint application light. Then stencil the leaves and stems Garden Green. Don't worry if some of the Garnet Red gets on the geranium leaves: This helps to tint the leaves, which adds depth to your painting. You may even tint other parts of the leaves with the Garnet Red brush.

4 Shade the geranium leaves with Basic Black and a ⅜-inch brush. Focus on areas where the leaves emerge from a stem or come from behind another leaf or flower. Remove the stencil, and wipe it clean.

5 Position and tape down the leaf detail overlay. Stencil the detail Christmas Green, and shade with a tiny bit of Basic Black and the ⅜-inch brush. Remove the overlay, and wipe it clean. Let the stencil crèmes dry completely.

6 To execute the second half of the image, flip the geranium stencil over and position the center blossom on top of the already-stenciled center blossom. *Do not restencil this flower or the one below it. They are strictly for registration. If you'd like, mask these flowers with an index card.* Tape the stencil in place.

7 Repeat steps 3–5 to stencil the second half of the geranium pattern.

8 If you need to stretch the design to fit the width of your shade, mask everything on the geranium stencil except the last 4 leaves. Position these leaves at both ends of the design,

Step 2

Step 6

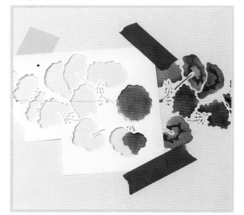

Step 8

adhere, and stencil. Don't forget the leaf detail! When the design is as long as you desire, add more flowers wherever you want using the individual blossom stencil.

9 Use the small petal stencil and Black Cherry paint to define each flower. Stencil these petals (or parts of them) in several places on each blossom, letting the petals extend beyond the edges of the blossom as well.

10 Finish by misting the stenciled area with at least 2 coats of spray varnish, letting it dry between coats.

Step 9

Geranium Window Shade
Variations

These geraniums can be bold and bright or soft and subtle. Work the stencil as much or as little as you like to create a rambling window "garden" or single flower motif. Create stripes of flowers, with or without the leaves, vertically or horizontally. Consider stenciling all or parts of the image on a floormat, picture frame, or towel hems. Brighten up any room in the house with this cheery design.

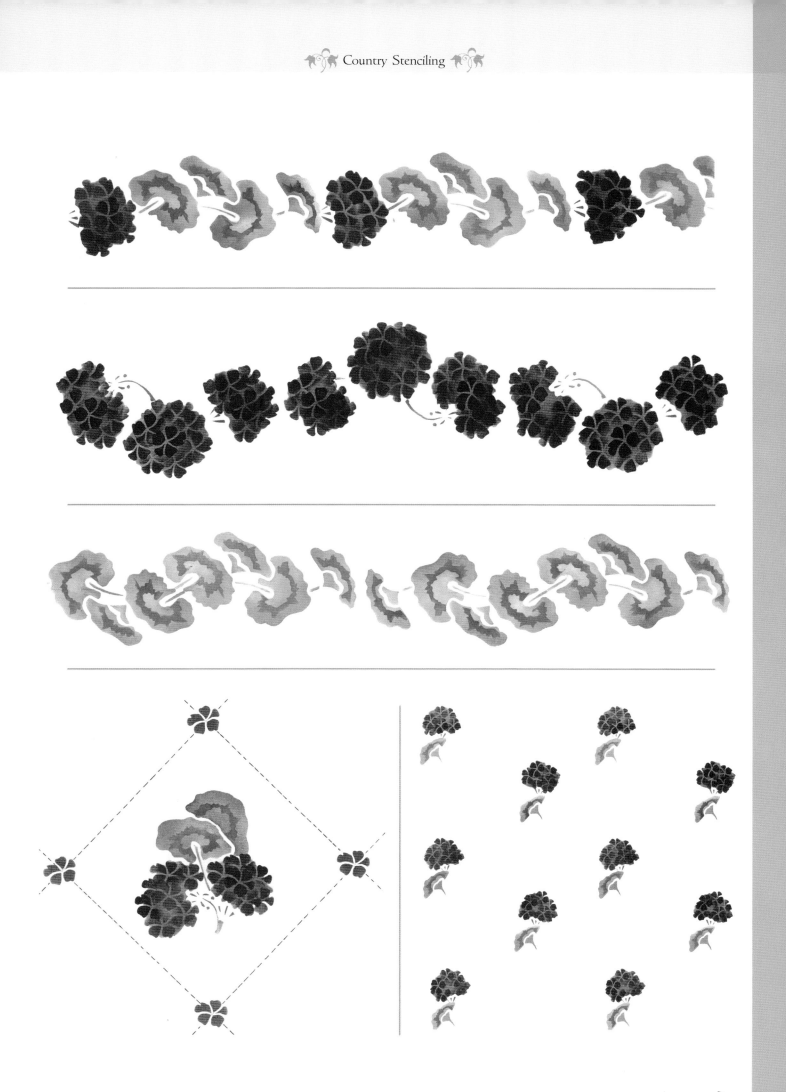

Country Crows
Mail Sorter

Classic country elements produce old-fashioned appeal in this easy project. You'll love the charm this country mail sorter delivers to your home.

WHAT YOU'LL NEED

- Unfinished mail sorter
- Delta Ceramcoat acrylic paint: Butter Cream, Candy Bar Brown
- Folk Art acrylic paint: English Mustard, Licorice
- 1-inch foam paintbrushes, 3
- ½-inch stencil brushes, 2
- ¼-inch stencil brushes, 2
- 1-inch flat paintbrushes, 2
- Antiquing gel
- Matte-finish brush-on varnish

Stencils for this project are located on page 111.

Trick of the Trade:
To make painting easier, twist out the mail sorter's hanging pegs and paint them separately.

1 Basecoat the mail sorter Butter Cream using a foam brush. Let dry, then paint the bottom, sides, and front panel Candy Bar Brown.

2 Center the "Mail" stencil on the front section of the sorter, and tape in place. Stencil English Mustard with a ½-inch brush.

3 Center the house/crows/star stencil on the back section of the mail sorter, and tape in place. Stencil the house Candy Bar Brown with a ½-inch brush, the chimney and crows Licorice (¼-inch brush), and the stars English Mustard (¼-inch brush).

4 Position the second overlay of the house stencil, tape in place, and stencil the roof, windows, and door Licorice. Stencil the star English Mustard with a ½-inch brush.

5 Place the checkerboard stencil along the top edge of the sorter, tape in place, and stencil Candy Bar Brown with a ½-inch brush. Move the stencil over, and repeat the checkerboard along the entire top edge of the sorter.

6 Using a flat brush and English Mustard, add detail along front edges of the mail sorter using light, feathered strokes.

7 To give the mail sorter an antiqued look, load a flat brush with antiquing gel. Gently offload the excess on a paper towel. Using a feather stroke and almost no pressure, work from the edges into the center to apply the gel. Let dry.

8 Brush on at least 1 coat of varnish to protect the mail sorter.

Step 2

Step 4

Step 6

Country Crows Mail Sorter
Variations

Traditional country style lasts through the ages with good reason. The crisp, graphic images look fresh and original whether rendered in dark or bold colors. Choose your favorite folk elements for a set of stacked bandboxes, a recipe box, or kitchen canisters. Create an enchanting country village simply by repeating the house motif in various colors.

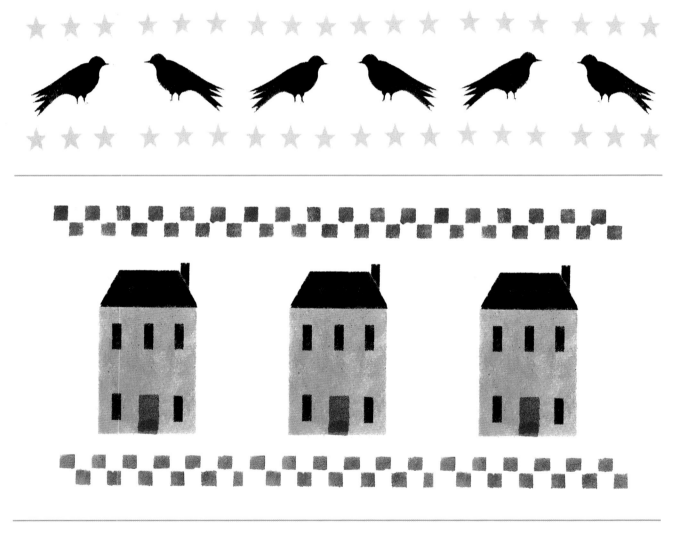

Teddy Bears
Border

Buttons and bears dance on the moon,
sending happy dreams and sweet slumber
to your little one.

WHAT YOU'LL NEED

- 4-inch sponge roller
- Delta Ceramcoat acrylic paint: Mello Yellow, White
- Delta Stencil Paint Crème: Cape Cod Blue, Goldenrod Yellow, Yellow Ochre, Amber, Bark Brown, Garnet Red, True Blue, Garden Green, Basic Black
- ¾-inch stencil brush
- ½-inch stencil brushes, 3
- ¼-inch stencil brushes, 5
- Index cards

Stencils for this project are located on page 113.

1 Measure and mark a horizontal pencil line on the wall for the top edge of the border. Measure down 7¼ inches from this line, and mark another pencil line to hold the border. Use low-adhesive tape to mask the outside edges of the border. Use a sponge roller to apply an even coat of Mello Yellow to the border. Leave tape in place.

Step 1

2 Position the diamond stencil on the wall with the top and bottom corners touching each edge of the border and aligned vertically. Tape in place.

Trick of the Trade: Put tape all the way around the stencil to keep it secure while stenciling and to prevent paint from going where it doesn't belong.

3 Using the sponge roller loaded with White, basecoat the diamond. Continue painting diamonds around the room, repositioning the stencil so the points of each diamond touch.

4 Reposition the stencil on each diamond, and stencil with Cape Cod Blue, using the ¾-inch brush and concentrating mainly on the edges.

5 Adhere the moon stencil in the center of the first diamond. Stencil the moon White. Repeat in each diamond.

Step 5

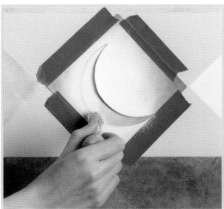

6 Reposition the moon stencil in the first diamond. Stencil the moon Goldenrod Yellow with a ½-inch brush. Shade the outside edges with Yellow Ochre. Repeat in each diamond.

7 There are 3 different bear stencils. Position one on each moon, alternating them in whatever order you like. Stencil the bears Amber (except for the ears, feet, and muzzle) using a ½-inch brush, and shade with Bark Brown and a ¼-inch brush. Stencil the ears, feet, and muzzle Bark Brown. Stencil the hanging bears' bows Garnet Red, the sitting bears' bows True Blue, and the sleeping bears' bows Garden Green. NOTE: Cover the moon with its dropout to protect it while stenciling the hanging bear's arm. Remove the moon dropout to expose the bear's paw,

Step 7

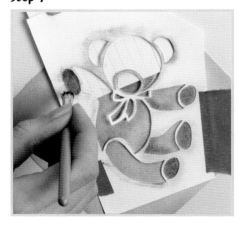

and mask the rest of the arm with an index card while stenciling the hand. (You may want to cut the index card to fit first.)

8 Position the open-eye face overlay on the sitting and hanging bear, and the closed-eye overlay on the sleeping bear, and carefully stencil the eyes, nose, and mouth Basic Black.

9 Place the button stencil at the point where 2 diamonds meet. Stencil the button White. Reposition and stencil buttons between each diamond. By the time you've stenciled all the buttons, the ones you started with will be dry. Starting at the beginning, reposition the stencil, and stencil the buttons Garnet Red, then shade lightly with Basic

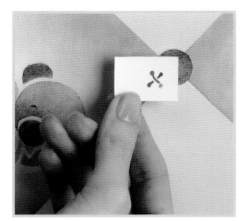

Step 9

Black. Once the red buttons are dry, place the overlay detail on top, and stencil with Basic Black.

Teddy Bears Border
Variations

Decorating a baby's room calls for all sorts of tiny touches. Just add these adorable bears to a chest of drawers, curtains, or cubbies. A simple moon with a cluster of buttons and a colorful ribbon may be all you need to embellish a toy chest or rocking chair. Whether you have a tiny nook or a wide-open wall to decorate, this design provides just the right touch of color and sweetness.

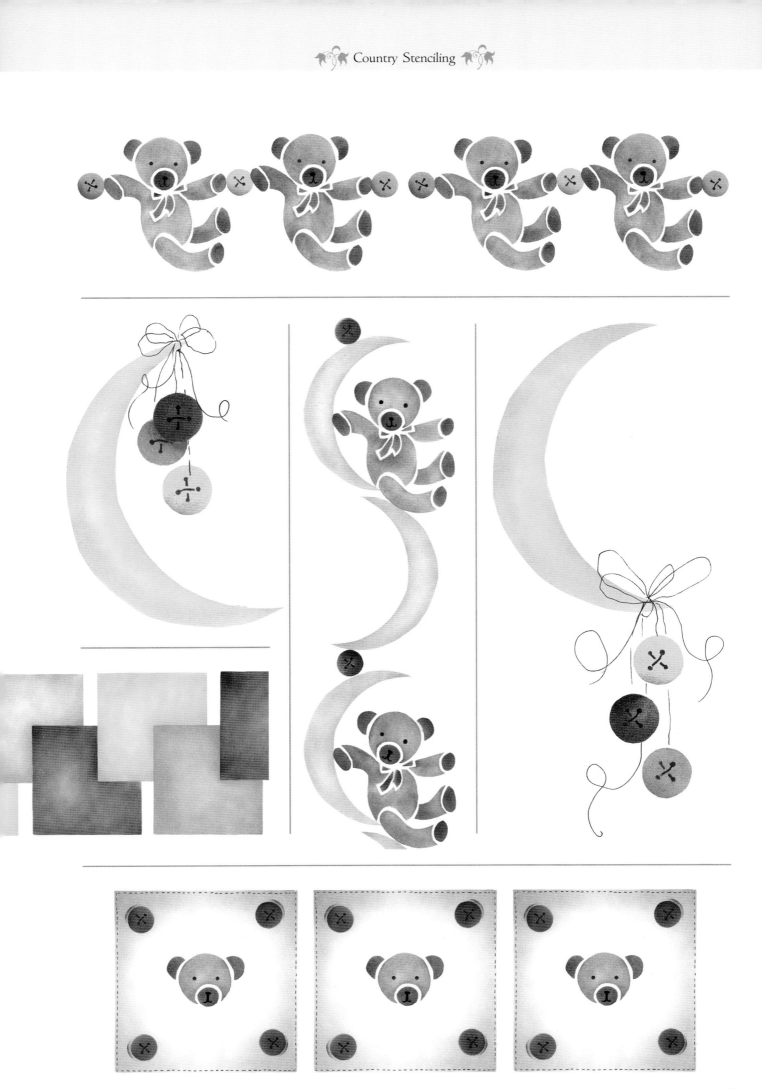

Country Cupboard

Display your collectibles against a picture-perfect backdrop! Your precious finds sparkle on the stage of this charming decorative cupboard.

WHAT YOU'LL NEED

- Americana acrylic paint: Jade Green
- Delta Ceramcoat acrylic paint: Gamal Green, Dark Burnt Umber, Berry Red, Burgundy Rose
- ⅝-inch stencil brush
- ⅜-inch stencil brushes, 3

Stencils for this project are located on page 115.

Trick of the Trade: As an alternative, you could also stencil pieces of this design directly onto the wood front of a piece of furniture. Just make sure to protect your finished work with spray varnish.

1 Measure and make a light pencil line on the wood behind the shelf. Mark the horizontal center of each stencil as well, and then line up stencil A with the pencil line on the wood. Position and tape down the stencil.

2 Basecoat the leaves Jade Green with the ⅝-inch brush, and shade the leaves with Gamal Green on a ⅜-inch brush. Stencil the berry stems Gamal Green with a ⅜-inch brush. Stencil the vine branch Dark Burnt Umber and the berries Berry Red, also with ⅜-inch brushes. Remove the stencil, and let dry completely.

3 Line up stencil B at the end of stencil A, and repeat step 2. Let dry.

4 Repeat steps 2 and 3 to stencil the vine-and-berry design across the width of the shelf.

5 Repeat steps 1–4 for each shelf area. For contrast, on the middle shelf basecoat the leaves with Burgundy Rose and shade them with Dark Burnt Umber. Then paint the berries Jade Green, and use Gamal Green for shading. The vine branch remains Dark Burnt Umber.

Step 1

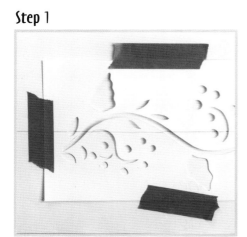

Step 2

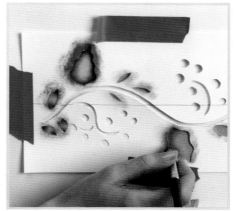

Step 3

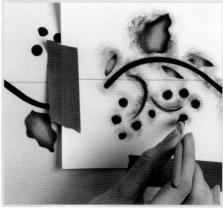

Country Cupboard
Variations

Add a hint of country loveliness with this winding vine of leaves and delicate berry sprays. Carry the look across the kitchen soffit, around a china saucer, or along a creamy linen tea towel. Change the stencil placement to twist the vine into a wreath or curve over an arched doorway. Alter the colors to suggest a variety of berries.

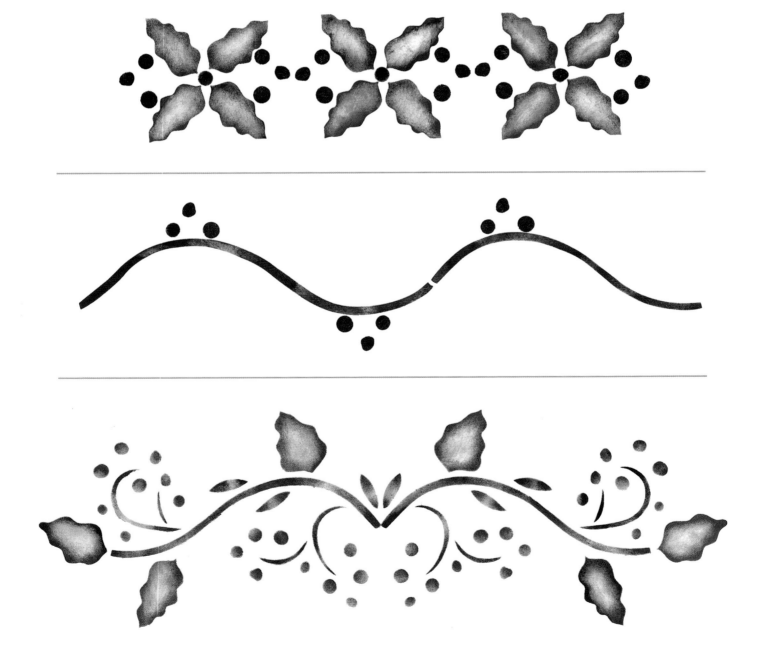

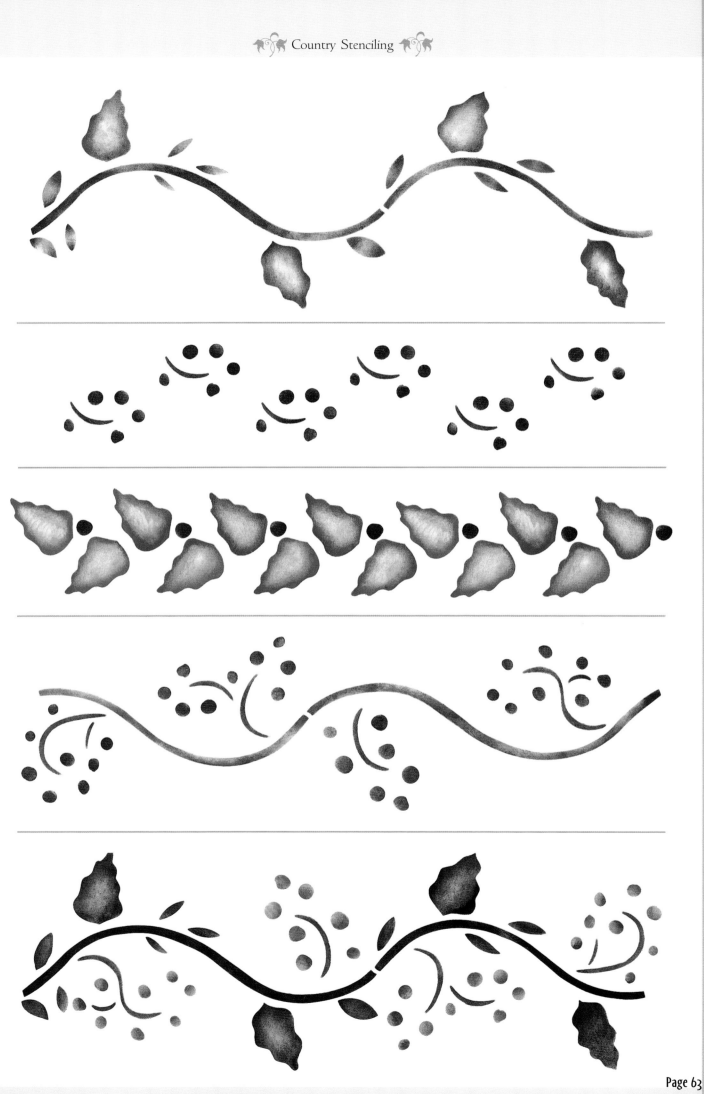

Sunflower
Pillows

*Cheery sunflowers and country checks
grace these inviting toss pillows. They offer country
comfort along with casual elegance.*

WHAT YOU'LL NEED

- Cardboard, 12 inches square
- Repositionable stencil adhesive
- 11-inch-square prewashed muslin
- Cardstock or heavyweight paper
- Scissors
- Delta Stencil Paint Crème: Sunflower Yellow, Amber, Bark Brown, Garden Green, Jungle Green, Basic Black, Sandstone, Colonial Green
- ⅝-inch stencil brushes, 2
- ⅜-inch stencil brushes, 6
- Disappearing-ink marking pen
- Iron-on adhesive
- Pillow, 12- to 14-inches square
- Brown fine-point permanent marker, optional

Stencils for this project are located on page 117.

Trick of the Trade: To further dress up the pillow, add your own freehand detail. To add lovely script, use a ruler and disappearing marking pen to mark lines 1 or 1½ inches apart in 2 of the squares. With the same pen, write the word "Sunflower" repeatedly on the lines, letting the words "hide" behind the flower petals and leaves. Trace over the words with brown permanent marker.

We also added faux stitching around the outline of the sunflower and the squares: To make straight lines, simply place a ruler where you want the stitching to be, and, using brown marker, draw a dashed line against it. For curved lines, carefully freehand the dashed lines.

1 Mist the cardboard square with repositionable stencil adhesive. Lay the muslin on the cardboard, and smooth it onto the sticky surface so the fabric will not move while stenciling.

2 Before you begin stenciling, you'll need to make a simple shield to protect the sunflower petals while you're stenciling the leaves. To do this, trace or stencil the outline of the sunflower onto a piece of cardstock or heavyweight paper. Lightly stencil the leaves as well, if you wish. Cut out the flower shield, and set it aside.

3 Position and adhere the large sunflower stencil in the center of the muslin square. Swirl Sunflower Yellow onto the petals, and stencil the center of the flower Amber with a ⅝-inch brush. Don't worry if some of the Amber gets on the petals; this will provide nice shading. Shade to the lower left and center of the petals with Bark Brown.

4 To stencil the leaves, first place the flower cutout from step 2 over the already-stenciled flower petals. Then use Garden Green and a ⅝-inch brush to fill in the leaves. Shade with Jungle Green and then very lightly with Basic Black. Remove the stencil and the flower cutout, and let dry.

5 Tape the small checkerboard stencil along one edge of the muslin square. Stencil the first row of checks along the edge of the muslin Basic Black, then lift the stencil and move it 1 square over and 1 row up to stencil the inside row of checks. Be sure the corners of the checks touch.

Step 2

Step 4

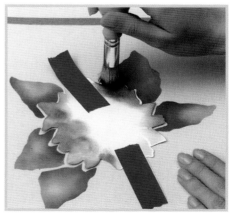

Repeat until the checkerboard is stenciled all the way around the muslin.

6 Divide the muslin square into 4 squares of roughly the same size, marking the lines lightly with a pencil and ruler. (Make sure you don't mark over the stenciled sunflower or the checked border.) Mask the flower and leaves with their dropouts. Mask off the upper left and lower

Step 6

right squares with tape, and stencil the remaining 2 squares Sandstone with a ⅝-inch brush. Let dry.

7 Remove the tape, and mask the Sandstone squares. Stencil the other 2 squares Colonial Green with a ⅝-inch brush, using a light, swirling motion to achieve a textured effect. Let dry.

8 Iron the stenciled muslin square onto a square of iron-on adhesive. Follow the manufacturer's directions to iron the muslin onto the pillow.

Sunflower Pillows
Variations

*W*ho says a sunflower has to be yellow? Change the palette to decorate walls for a teenager who loves candy-colored daisies. Use them to make a swag along the edge of a bed skirt, curtains, or perhaps a bed canopy with stenciled flowers scattered on sheer fabric. Checkerboards of all sizes mix and match with this design, whether creating quilt patterns or connecting the flowers in a border of blooms.

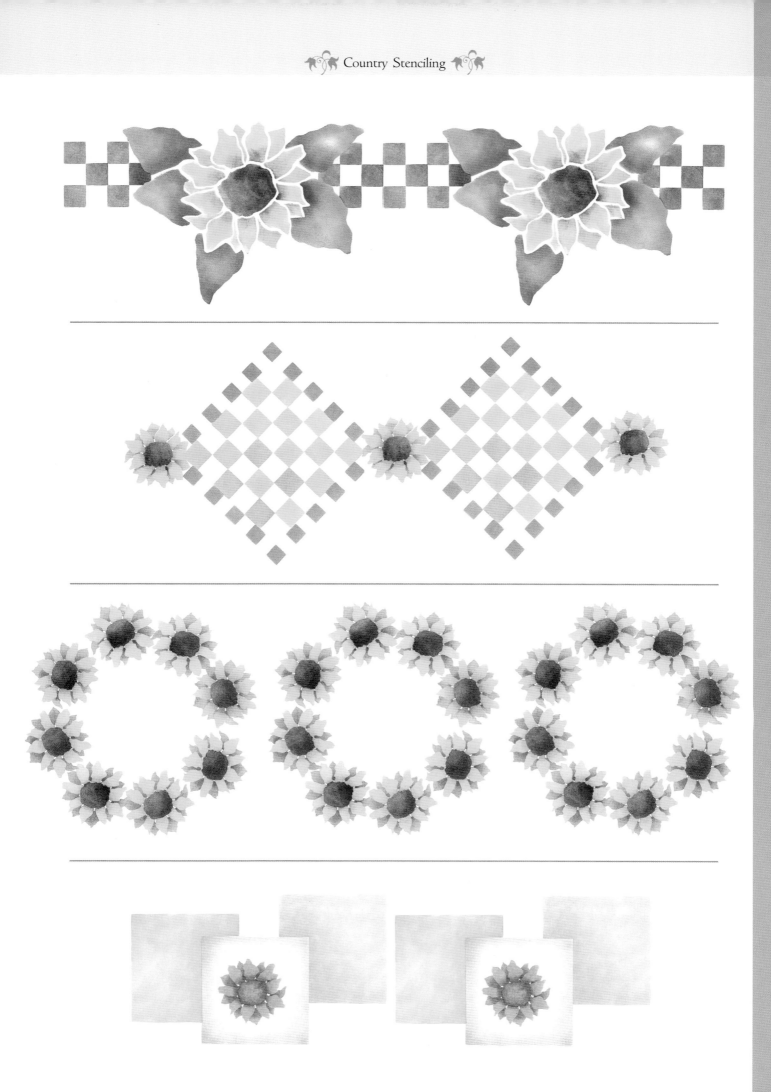

Country Birdhouse
Cabinet

*Birdhouse lovers (and everyone else!)
will flock to this downhome cabinet—
a showstopper in any setting.*

Trick of the Trade: For an antiqued look, before you begin, distress the cabinet by sanding it with a fine- to medium-grade sandpaper, rubbing off some but not all of the paint. Seal with a wood sealer, then basecoat with Antique White. Repeat the process, using Light Ivory this time. Sand one last time.

WHAT YOU'LL NEED

- White 2-door cabinet, approximately 18×24 inches
- Sandpaper
- Wood sealer
- Delta Ceramcoat acrylic paint: Antique White, Light Ivory
- Delta Stencil Paint Crème: Garden Green, Basic Black, Dark Barn Red, Amber, Navy Blue
- 1-inch flat brush
- ½-inch stencil brushes, 5
- Art gum eraser
- Index cards
- Matte-finish spray varnish

Stencils for this project are located on page 119.

1 Begin by stenciling the leafy branches, referring to the photo to determine placement. Secure the stencil with tape, and swirl Garden Green on the leaves, varying the intensity of the color. Shade with Basic Black, and tint with a tiny bit of Dark Barn Red. Use Amber on the

stems. Reposition until all the branches have been stenciled on the front and sides of the cabinet.

2 Refer to the photo to determine placement of the birdhouses as well. Secure the large birdhouse stencil on the left door of the cabinet, and stencil with Dark Barn Red. Shade around the edges with Basic Black, and apply Basic Black to the roof and the circular opening.

3 To make the post, place 2 pieces of low-adhesive tape about an inch apart directly under the black circle, extending from the birdhouse to the bottom of the cabinet. Stencil the post Amber, making the edges darker than the middle. Add

some additional shading with Basic Black under the birdhouse and along the edges.

4 Before you reposition the large birdhouse stencil "behind" the red house, use low-adhesive tape to mask off the top of the red birdhouse. Stencil the second house Navy Blue, and shade around the edges with Basic Black. Also stencil the opening Basic Black. Stencil the roof Amber. Let dry.

5 Hold down the star stencil on the blue house, and erase the paint within the stars with the art gum eraser. Repeat until you're pleased with the star design. (Note: This technique works only with paint crème, not acrylics.)

Step 3

Step 4

Step 5

Step 6

6 "Hang" the blue house from a branch by creating a stripe stencil. Tape 2 index cards ⅛ inch apart. Drag Basic Black over stripe.

7 Tape the small birdhouse stencil to the right of the blue birdhouse, and stencil it Amber. Shade with Basic Black. Stencil the roof Navy Blue and the opening Basic Black. Repeat step 6 to create a "wire."

8 Stencil the next small house in the same manner, using Dark Barn Red and Basic Black.

9 Stencil the big birdhouse on the right Amber, and shade with Basic Black. Stencil the roof Navy Blue and the opening Basic Black. While the stencil is still in place, tape down the checkerboard stencil at the top of the birdhouse sides. Stencil the checks Dark Barn Red, then reposition the stencil to paint the second and fourth rows of checks. Be sure the corners of the checks touch. Repeat the checkerboard at the bottom edge of the birdhouse, but stencil only 3 rows of checks here. Repeat step 6 to "hang" this birdhouse from the branch above it.

10 Cover the checkered hanging house with its dropout to protect it, and stencil a small house below it Navy Blue. Shade with Basic Black, and use Dark Barn Red for the roof and Basic Black for the opening. Repeat step 6 to "hang" this birdhouse from the checkered house.

11 To stencil the wren, position the body overlay in the branches at the bottom right of the cabinet, mark the registration points, and stencil with Amber. Add shading with Basic Black. Position the second overlay, and stencil with Basic Black.

12 Mist the entire surface with at least 2 coats of spray varnish. (Let dry between coats.) Then lightly load a brush with Amber and offload on a paper towel. Brush color lightly along the edges of the cabinet. Wipe away excess paint with a paper towel. Apply 2 more coats of spray varnish. Let dry.

Country Birdhouse Cabinet
Variations

Bring the outdoors in with your own engaging birdhouse variations. Add them to room dividers, sisal mats, or cupboards to brighten an all-season sunroom. Stretch your style and stencil checkerboards, leaves, and wrens wherever they are inclined to perch. Mix and match for color and style. Antique them to add an aged look. The fun is all yours—the sky's the limit.

Zinnia Garden
Border

Sweet smiles bloom every day in this blissfully sunny summer garden designed for a princess.

Trick of the Trade: To get the perfect colors for the wall, select your favorite craft paints and take them into a paint store, where you can have latex paint mixed for a perfect match.

WHAT YOU'LL NEED

- Light Ivory latex wall paint
- 4-inch sponge roller
- Delta Ceramcoat acrylic paint: Mello Yellow
- Delta Stencil Paint Crème: Cottage Blue, Navy Blue, Garden Green, Basic Black, Goldenrod Yellow, Amber, Coral, Garnet Red, Amethyst Purple, Paprika
- ½-inch stencil brushes, 6
- ¼-inch stencil brushes, 4

Stencils for this project are located on page 121.

1 Basecoat the wall with satin- or eggshell-finish Light Ivory latex wall paint.

2 To create 4-inch stripes around the room, use a plumb line or a level to extend lines from the ceiling to the floor at 4-inch intervals around the room. (Make sure the lines are 4 inches apart at both the ceiling and the floor.) Mask off both sides of *every other* stripe with tape.

Trick of the Trade: To avoid painting a wrong stripe, put a small piece of tape in the stripes you will not paint.

3 Use the sponge roller to roll Mello Yellow onto every other stripe. Be careful to stay within the taped area. Let dry.

4 Make as many flowers as you like around the base of the wall, stenciling them at different heights and with different colors. Before you begin, plan your design and make a pencil mark to indicate the placement of each flower, varying flower placement so as not to create a pattern.

5 Each flower has 3 overlays: Work with the overlay with the largest open areas first. Position this stencil on the wall, and tape it to secure. Mark the registration points. Stencil each zinnia in the same manner, referring to the chart on the next page for color. Apply the basecoat first, then shade with a darker value.

Petals: Stencil the basecoat darker toward the center and

Step 3

lighter at the tips with a ½-inch brush. Swirl on the darker shading with a ¼-inch brush.

Center: Stencil color with a ½-inch brush, and shade along the left curve with a ¼-inch brush.

Leaves: Stencil Garden Green with a ½-inch brush, making the color darker where each leaf emerges from the stem and along the bottom. Add a tiny bit of Basic Black shading with a ¼-inch brush. Apply light tints of Paprika (½-inch brush) and Garnet Red (¼-inch brush).

6 Position the second overlay by matching the registration points. Tape it down securely, then stencil the petals as you did in step 5. Stencil the stem Garden

Step 5

Green, adding a little Garnet Red at the point where the flower touches the stem. If you've positioned the flower particularly high on the wall, the stem will not reach the baseboard. If this is the case, just slide the stencil down to fill the gap.

7 Position and tape the third overlay in place, and stencil the petals in the same manner as before. Stencil the vein lines Garden Green, and darken slightly with Garnet Red.

8 Before stenciling the bumblebees, decide where they will go and make a light pencil mark at

Step 6

each position. Vary their placement throughout the zinnias.

9 Adhere the first overlay (the one without wings) to the wall, and mark the registration points. Stencil with Basic Black.

10 Position and tape down the bumblebee overlay. Stencil the stripes Goldenrod

Step 10

Yellow (½-inch brush) and the wings, legs, and antennae Basic Black (½-inch brush). Apply paint sparingly to the wings so they look soft and a bit transparent. Shade the edges of the stripes with a small amount of Basic Black on a ¼-inch brush. Repeat steps 9 and 10 for all bumblebees.

ZINNIA COLOR PALETTE

Blue Zinnia	Yellow Zinnia	Pink Zinnia	Purple Zinnia	Green Zinnia	Orange Zinnia
Basecoat: Cottage Blue	*Basecoat: Goldenrod Yellow*	*Basecoat: Coral*	*Basecoat: Amethyst Purple*	*Basecoat: Garden Green*	*Basecoat: Paprika*
Shading: Navy Blue	*Shading: Amber*	*Shading: Garnet Red*	*Shading: Basic Black*	*Shading: Basic Black*	*Shading: Amber*
Center: Goldenrod Yellow	*Center: Garden Green*	*Center: Goldenrod Yellow*	*Center: Goldenrod Yellow*	*Center: Coral*	*Center: Goldenrod Yellow*
Center shading: Amber	*Center shading: Garnet Red*	*Center shading: Amber*	*Center shading: Amber*	*Center shading: Garnet Red*	*Center shading: Amber*

Zinnia Garden Border
Variations

Get out your paint set, because zinnias come in any color. And since they're the hardy variety, they bloom almost anywhere! Picture them on toy boxes, dresser drawers, or jewelry boxes. Stencil just the petals on pine floors, or make a border of leaves along the edge of the ceiling. Try the bees and little button flowers in smaller places. Create borders and stripes to turn the room into a field of dreams.

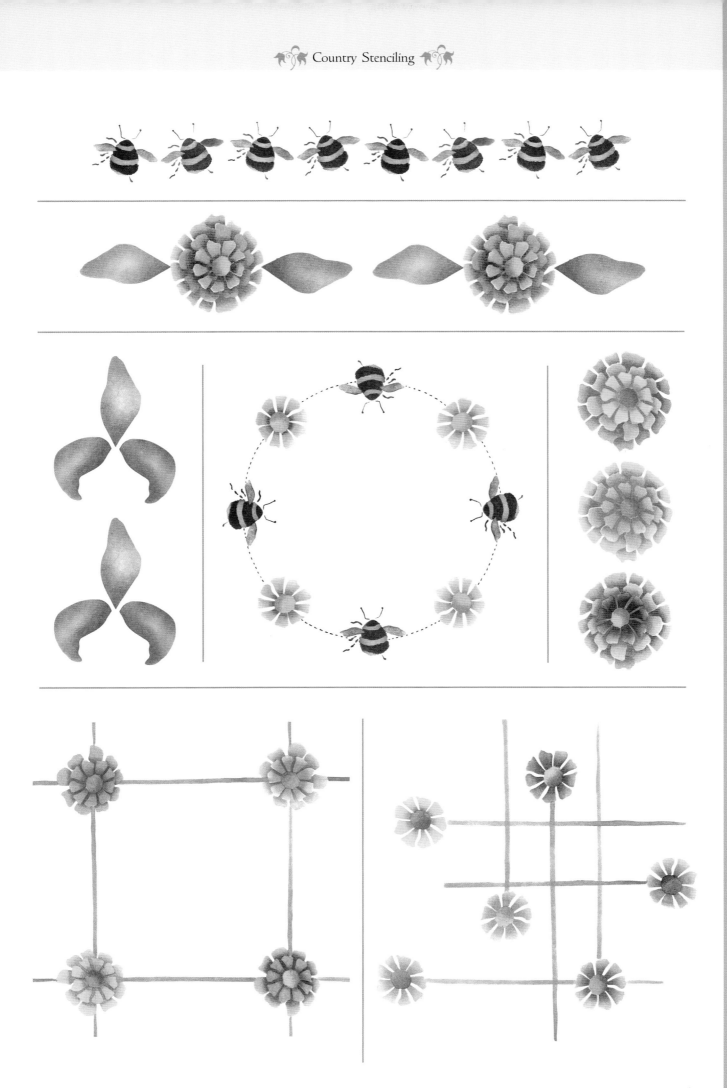

Skill level: Intermediate
Time: 1½ hours per place mat

Rooster
Table Linens

Set your table with country sentiment and vibrant style. These delightful roosters will give you something to crow about at every meal!

WHAT YOU'LL NEED

- Fabric medium
- Fabric place mat
- Delta Ceramcoat acrylic paint: Maple Sugar Tan, Brown Iron Oxide, Burgundy Rose
- Americana acrylic paint: Hauser Dark Green
- Folk Art acrylic paint: Blue Ink
- ¾-inch stencil brush
- ⅝-inch stencil brushes, 4

Stencils for this project are located on page 123.

1 Before stenciling, follow the manufacturer's instructions to add fabric medium to the acrylic paint.

2 Position the large rooster stencil in the center of the place mat. Tape it in place. Mark the corner registration points on pieces of tape on the mat.

3 Basecoat the rooster's body and the base of the tail feathers (where the feathers attach to the body) Maple Sugar Tan with the ¾-inch brush. Let dry, then shade with Brown Iron Oxide on a ⅝-inch brush.

4 Beginning at the base of the tail feathers and working along the length of the feathers, stencil the colors in the following order on ⅝-inch brushes: Brown Iron Oxide, Hauser Dark Green, Blue Ink, and Burgundy Rose. Slightly overlap the colors where they meet each other. Stencil the neck feathers from the head down in the same order, leaving out the Burgundy Rose at the end.

5 Basecoat the rooster's legs, feet, comb, beak, and wattle Burgundy Rose. Remove the first overlay, and let dry.

6 Tape the second overlay in place. Repeat step 4 to stencil the additional neck feathers. Stipple Brown Iron Oxide on the eye and feather detail. Remove the overlay.

7 To stencil the border, line up the stencil along a short edge of the place mat. Tape in place. Stencil the center row of the border Burgundy Rose, letting the paint overlap onto the outer rows of triangles as well. Stencil the outer triangles Blue Ink, slightly blending the 2 colors. Move the stencil along the edge of the place mat, and repeat until

Step 6

Step 3

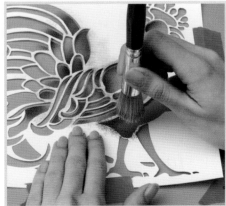

Step 4

Step 7

the border covers the entire edge. Repeat for the other short edge.

8 Once the short edges are complete, use tape to mask off the corners of the short edges, and repeat step 7 to stencil the border on the long edges of the place mat.

9 When the paint is completely dry, place a soft, clean cloth over the design and run an iron over the cloth to heat-set the paint.

Rooster Table Linens
Variations

Center the rooster as a stand-alone design on a chair seat or serving tray. Alter the colors to fit in with any decorating scheme. Add the geometric border (in any color combination, of course) to backsplash tiles to extend the motif into the rest of the room, or accent candlesticks and napkin rings with a bit of border detail to complete the table scene.

Vintage Floral
Tablecloth

*A trailing garland of flowers
and foliage adds country nostalgia to
a charming bedside table.*

WHAT YOU'LL NEED

- Large piece of paper, at least as big as the tabletop surface
- Iron
- Disappearing-ink marking pen or chalk pencil
- Fabric tablecloth
- Straight pins (optional)
- Repositionable stencil adhesive
- Fabric medium
- Index cards
- Delta Ceramcoat acrylic paint: Green Sea, Sachet Pink, Berry Red
- Americana acrylic paint: Hauser Dark Green
- ⅜-inch stencil brushes, 4

  Stencils for this project are located on page 125.

 Because your table may be a different size than the table shown here, follow these directions for adapting the stencil design to your needs. First, make a paper template of the tabletop. Fold the template in half, then in

Trick of the Trade: This design would also look lovely painted directly onto a round wooden table.

half again to create quarters. Then fold it in half once again. Unfold. You will have 8 equal pie-shape sections. Set aside until step 3.

2 Measure and mark the center of the stencil. Draw a pencil mark at this point to divide the design in half.

3 To get an idea of how the design will translate onto your tabletop, practice on the paper template instead of proceeding directly to the fabric. Position the stencil on the edge of the paper template, aligning the pencil line with a fold line on the template. Tape the stencil in place, with the flower toward the center of the template.

 When planning the spacing, first trace the entire stencil

on *every other* fold line. After seeing how much space there is between each stencil design, you can determine which part or parts of the design you wish to use to fill the space attractively. Here, the stencil has been turned upside down, with only the ferns at the bottom traced onto the remaining fold lines.

5 Now fold the tablecloth as you did the template. This time, use an iron to lightly press each fold to create the 8 equal sections. Or, lightly mark each fold line with a disappearing marking pen or a chalk pencil.

6 Center the paper template on the fabric, and tape it in place. Outline the edge of the circle with either a chalk pencil or

Step 1

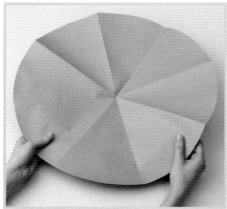

Step 2

Step 6

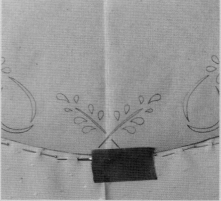

straight pins. Remove the tape and the template.

7 Mist a piece of cardboard with repositionable stencil adhesive. Lay the fabric on the cardboard, and smooth it onto the sticky surface to keep it from slipping while you stencil.

8 Before you begin stenciling, mix each of the paint colors with a fabric medium according to the manufacturer's directions.

9 Center the stencil at the edge of the circle on one of the fold lines, and tape in place. Stencil the leaves and stems Green Sea and the flowers Sachet Pink. Shade the green areas with

Step 9

Hauser Dark Green; use Berry Red for shading the pink areas.

10 Place the stencil upside down in the center of the next fold. Tape in place. Use index cards or tape to mask off everything but the ferns at the bottom of the stencil. Stencil the leaves and stems Green Sea, and shade with Hauser Dark Green.

Step 10

11 Repeat steps 9 and 10 until all 8 fold lines have been stenciled.

12 Allow the paint to dry thoroughly, then remove the cardboard from the back of the fabric. When the paint is completely dry, place a soft, clean cloth over the design and run an iron over the cloth to heat-set the paint.

Vintage Floral Tablecloth
Variations

W *hile soft greens and pinks bespeak romance, a change of colors is all that's required to alter the feel of this design. Try country blue and dusty rose to invoke a warm, peaceful aura. Experiment by rearranging the stylish elements of this stencil to add a coordinated touch throughout the room. Frame your headboard, trim a picture frame, place a ring of flowers around the ceiling fixture: Your choices are endless, and the look is ageless.*

A Parade of
Keepsake Boxes

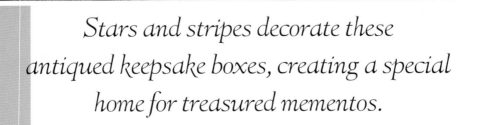

*Stars and stripes decorate these
antiqued keepsake boxes, creating a special
home for treasured mementos.*

WHAT YOU'LL NEED

- 3 papier mâché boxes: 3-inch star, 4-inch hexagon, 5-inch hexagon
- Folk Art acrylic paint: Butter Pecan
- Delta Ceramcoat acrylic paint: Blue Velvet
- Americana acrylic paint: Antique Maroon
- 1-inch foam paintbrushes, 3
- ½-inch stencil brushes, 3
- 1-inch flat paintbrushes, 3
- ¼-inch stencil brush
- Antiquing gel
- Matte-finish brush-on varnish

Stencils for this project are located on page 127.

3-INCH STAR BOX

1 Basecoat the box Butter Pecan, top of lid Blue Velvet, and sides of lid Antique Maroon with foam brushes. Let dry; repeat.

2 Position the thin stripe stencil along the edge of the lid, and tape in place. With a ½-inch brush, stencil this border Antique Maroon. Repeat the stripe on each of the star's edges.

3 Position the small stars stencil on the lid, and stencil Butter Pecan with a ½-inch brush. Repeat to create a pleasing design.

4-INCH HEXAGON BOX

1 Basecoat the box Blue Velvet, top of lid Butter Pecan, and sides of lid Antique Maroon with foam brushes. Let dry; repeat.

2 Position the thick stripe stencil across the top of the lid, and stencil Blue Velvet with a ½-inch brush. Repeat across lid.

3 Repeat step 2 from the star box to stencil an Antique Maroon border around the lid.

4 Lightly load a flat brush with Butter Pecan, and brush the edges of the box, applying very little pressure. (This will highlight the lines of the box.)

5 Measure and mark the center of each side panel of the box. Working on one panel at a time, position the circular stars/1776 stencil on the mark and tape in place. Stencil with Butter Pecan and a ¼-inch brush. Repeat on each panel.

5-INCH HEXAGON BOX

1 Basecoat the box Antique Maroon, top of lid Antique Maroon, and sides of lid Blue Velvet with foam brushes. Let dry; repeat.

2 Repeat step 2 from the star box to stencil a Blue Velvet border around the lid.

3 Center the large star stencil on the lid, tape in place, and stencil with Butter Pecan and a ½-inch brush.

4 Lightly load a flat brush with Butter Pecan, and softly

Step 2—Star box

Step 4—4-inch hexagon

Step 5—5-inch hexagon

brush the edges of the lid to create a highlight.

5 Measure and mark the center of each side panel of the box. Working on one panel at a time, position the medium-size star on the mark and tape in place. Stencil with Butter Pecan on a ½-inch brush. Repeat on each panel.

6 Load a flat brush with Blue Velvet, and lightly brush the edges of the box.

FINISHING

1 Load a flat brush with antiquing gel, and gently offload the excess on a paper towel. Using a feather stroke and almost no pressure, apply antiquing gel to all the painted pieces. Let dry.

2 Brush on matte-finish varnish to seal the paint.

A Parade of Keepsake Boxes
Variations

Add classic Americana style to your favorite home accessories with stars and stripes in patriotic colors. This motif works well in any room and on practically any surface. Try embellishing a family room fireplace screen, a table runner, or a desktop. Imagine the 1776 circle of stars as an unusual clock face. To enhance the weathered look, keep the palette dark and apply a crackle-finish or antiquing medium.

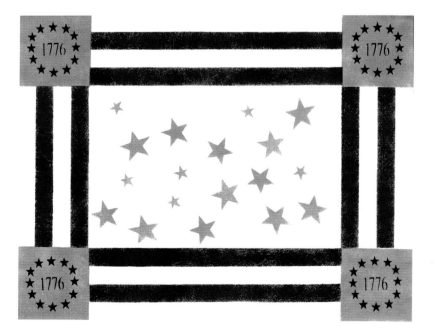

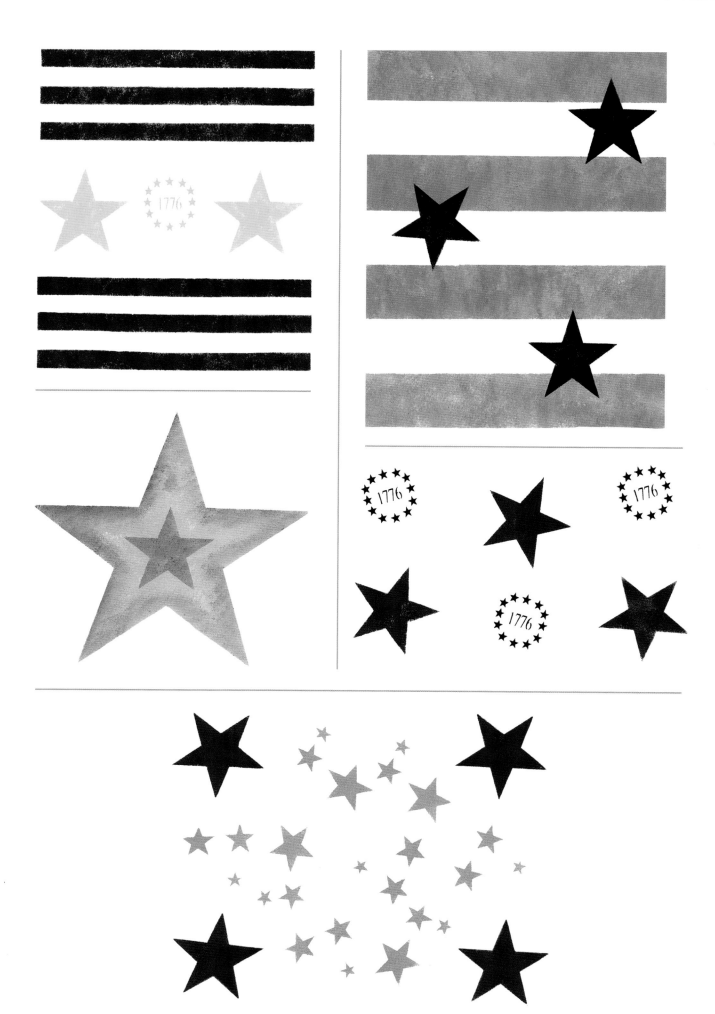

Resource Directory

Listed below are the names and numbers of the stencils used in this book. Some stencils have been adjusted to fit the size parameters of this book.

The Robins & Willoughby Collection at L.A. Stencilworks

Seed-Packet Pots, page 12
#2241 Mini Stuff
#752 Gardeners' Seed Packets with Holder

Farmhouse Plate & Shelf, page 16
#3171 Blank Scallop Plate
#3089 Jarred Johnson Collection

Flowers & Ivy Nook, page 20
#609 Mix & Match Stem and Filler Flower Separates
#614 Ivy Separates III

French Country Kitchen, page 32
#2786 Blank Tiles
#3101 Mexican Tile Designs
#216 French Panel Inset

Rustic Moose Lampshade, page 40
#2490 Lodge Vignette II - Moose
#2808 Western Vignette Mini Elements

Country Cupboard, page 60
#3082 Folk Art Kit II

Rooster Table Linens, page 76
#2405 French Rooster
#3075 Folk Art Borders I

Vintage Floral Tablecloth, page 80
#231 Hanging Flower Panel

Catalogs, stencils, paints, and stenciling supplies are available to order:
L.A. Stencilworks
16115 Vanowen St.
Van Nuys, CA 91406
Toll free: (877) 989-0262
Fax: (818) 989-0405
http://www.lastencil.com
E-mail: lastencil@lastencil.com

Stencils by Nancy

(Please note: Additional stencils are listed below that coordinate nicely with those featured in this book.)

Barnyard Animals Chair, page 24
#LB84c Chicken Wire
#GS51 Checkerboard Stencil
#GS12 Pig, Pig
#GS13 Sheep
#GS15 Pete the Rabbit
#GS16 Liz the Rabbit
#GS37 Toy Truck
#GS79 Tractor

Bountiful Fruit Buckets, page 28
#LB10 Apple
#LB34 Pear
#GSG49 Grapes
#GS51 Checkerboard
#LB83 Lemon
#LB32 Orange
#LB33 Cherries

Garden Butterfly Border, page 36
#LB01 Straight Grapevine
#LB44 Three Little Leaves
#GC16 Butterfly Border
#GSG42 Butterfly
#GC07 Creative Grapevine Wreath
#GSG70 Dragon Fly
#GSG55 Bumble Bee

Geranium Window Shade, page 48
#GSG08 Geraniums

Teddy Bears Border, page 56
#GS38 Teddy Bear
#GS39 Sheep Pull Toy
#GS40 Horse Pull Toy
#GS41 Rag Doll
#GS86 Grant the Bear
#GS87 Kaylee the Bunny
#BB02-BB06 Whimsy Moons & Stars

Sunflower Pillows, page 64
#GS51, GS52 Checkerboard
#GSG35 Sunflowers

Country Birdhouse Cabinet, page 68
#GSG13 Two Story Birdhouse
#GS50 Checkerboard
#GSG38 Wren
#GSG22 Leaf Branch
#GSG11 Birdhouse
#GSG10 Cottage Birdhouse
#GSG14 Swingin' Birdhouse

Zinnia Garden Border, page 72
#GSG41 Zinnia
#GSG55 Bumble Bee

Catalogs and stencils are available to order:
Stencils by Nancy
15219 Stuebner Airline,
   Suites 9–10
Houston, TX 77069
Phone: (281) 893-2227
Fax: (281) 893-3232
http://www.stencilsbynancy.net
E-mail:
stennan@stencilsbynancy.net

Primitive Designs

Welcome Friends Hallway, page 44
(Stencils by Leanne Watson; execution by Nancy Tribolet.)

Country Crows Mail Sorter, page 52

A Parade of Keepsake Boxes, page 84

Stencils are sold in sets, but custom orders can be created. Finished items are also available.
Primitive Designs
RR 3 Box 529
Spencer, IN 47460
Phone: (812) 876-3473
Fax: (812) 935-7652
http://www.primitivedesigns.com
E-mail: LW@primitivedesigns.com

Seed-Packet Pots See pages 12–15 for instructions.

tomatoes

radishes

carrots